The King's Ambassador

The King's Ambassador

Thomas Cranmer

David Luckman

CF4·K

10 9 8 7 6 5 4 3 2 1

Copyright © 2022 David Luckman
Paperback ISBN: 978-1-5271-0877-6
Ebook ISBN: 978-1-5271-0957-5

Published by Christian Focus Publications,
Geanies House, Fearn, Tain, Ross-shire,
IV20 1TW, Scotland, U.K.
www.christianfocus.com;
email: info@christianfocus.com

Cover design by Daniel van Straaten
Cover illustration by Daniel van Straaten
Printed and bound by Nørhaven, Denmark

Contents

The Dinner Party

Freedom is a precious thing. To have it taken away is a terrible tragedy. Thomas Cranmer thought he was a free man that September day in 1553. The journey from Lambeth Palace to the Palace of Westminster in London, England, would only take about fifteen minutes by foot. As the weather was fair, he thought he might leave the horse in the stable and walk. Thomas had been summoned to appear before the judges of the Star Chamber. It was a court in England, set up to hear cases of people who held influential positions in society, without the judges being intimidated by the defendants high status in life.

His wife, Margarete, had a look of fear in her eyes. 'Do not worry, my dear,' said Thomas softly, taking her hands. 'I will be ok.' He brought her hands to his lips and kissed them. 'The good Lord is with me,' he said. 'What can they do to me? As our Lord Christ Jesus said in Matthew's Gospel, "do not fear those who kill the body but cannot kill the soul. Rather fear him who can destroy both soul and body in hell."' He smiled.

Since Mary had ascended to the throne of England. Thomas knew that he might be a target for the Queen of England's anger.

Thomas had been the Archbishop of Canterbury in England for twenty years. He was a clever man – a gentle and kind man. Thomas loved God. He loved the Bible. He loved people and he loved prayer. Thomas knew from his study of the Scriptures, that those who follow Christ will suffer for His name. He was a man of God, an ambassador of Christ the King. He prayed that the Lord would grant him the strength and courage to continue the fight against sin, the world, and the devil, even if that fight took away his freedom, or his life.

Archbishop Cranmer arrived at the Palace of Westminster and was led swiftly to the Star Chamber. The doors opened and Thomas was ushered in. He was directed to stand before the judges.

'My Lord Archbishop,' said the leading judge. 'We are grateful that you have come. We are concerned that you have written reproachful comments regarding the Latin Mass. And the queen is most perplexed. What say you?'

'It was never my intention to have my statement copied and distributed across London in the way it was. I am sorry that it passed from my hands into the hands of another bishop. He then had numerous copies made. Whereas I had planned to pin it to the door of St Paul's, and to other church doors around the city, with my own episcopal seal on it.'

'Your intention matters not. However, your words do. I am instructed to charge you with treason against the Crown. You will be incarcerated in the Tower of London immediately. Guards!'

The archbishop was shocked and could hardly get a word out in his defence. A group of guards armed with long pikes rushed to his side and roughly restrained him. Then Thomas was frogmarched out of the Chamber and pushed into an armoured carriage that was waiting outside. The three-mile journey to the Tower of London was very uncomfortable over bumpy roads. Thomas would have to get used to being uncomfortable. The cells in the Tower were dark and dank. Not very comfortable at all. Once there, the guards grabbed Thomas by the arms and pulled him out of the carriage. They bundled him along the pathways to his cell. Once inside, they removed his restraints.

'Make yourself at home,' said the jailer dryly, as he closed the cell door. 'You'll be here a while.'

Thomas walked to the wall that was farthest from the cell door and sat down on the cold stone floor. He closed his eyes and cast his mind back to the time when it all started – when his life as a Cambridge don changed forever. Little did Thomas know that when he finished the evening meal at the Cressy home in Waltham, Essex, he would begin the journey to the highest position in the Church of England. He didn't desire to be Archbishop of Canterbury. He was a lowly professor of divinity at Jesus College in Cambridge.

And he liked it that way. He loved his college and his students. He thought that he would remain there long into his dotage. He had no aspirations to join the ranks of elite gentry in the king's court. And he wasn't interested in making a name for himself in the Anglican Church.

The plague drove him to the safe sanctuary of the Cressy home on 2nd August 1529. Like his college colleagues back in Cambridge, Thomas wanted to put as much distance between him and the plague as quickly as possible. He arrived with the two Cressy boys at their home. The boys were receiving tuition from Thomas at his Cambridge university, and he wanted to bring them home to their father in Waltham.

The travellers received a hearty welcome from Mr and Mrs Cressy. 'Dr Cranmer, it is so good to see you!' declared Mr Cressy. The boys were being squeezed tightly by their mother. 'Welcome to our home.'

'You are most kind, Mr Cressy,' replied Thomas. 'Things are a little dire in the city with the return of the plague. I am very grateful to you and Mrs Cressy for your hospitality.'

'Not at all,' said Mr Cressy. 'Let's get you to your room. Dinner will be served shortly, Dr Cranmer.'

After settling into his quarters, Thomas made his way to the dining room. He could hear familiar voices resonating from the other side of the door. Thomas turned the handle and walked into the room. The pleasant aroma of roast chicken and cooked vegetables filled his nostrils as he entered.

Mr and Mrs Cressy were sitting at the table with the two boys. Then he noticed his friends seated beside them. Dr Edward Fox and Dr Stephen Gardiner sat opposite each other at the dining room table.

'Well, if it isn't my old friends, Dr Fox and Dr Gardiner!' exclaimed Thomas jovially. The men stood and shook Thomas's hand vigorously.

'Dr Cranmer, what a pleasant surprise,' said Edward Fox.

'What brings you here?' asked Stephen Gardiner, as the three men sat down at the table. All three were educated in Cambridge, although at different universities. Stephen Gardiner and Edward Fox were in the service of King Henry VIII. And both men were at their wits end concerning the king's 'Great Matter' – his divorce from his wife, Queen Catherine of Aragon.

'You will have heard that the plague is back,' Thomas remarked. 'This time it is in Cambridge. Therefore, I am taking some time away from my college until it is safe to return.'

'Very wise,' said Stephen.

The conversation at the table was easy and at times jovial. When the meal was over, the Cressy family bade them all a goodnight and went off to bed. Once the door of the dining room closed behind them, the conversation between the three men continued with a more serious tone.

'I wasn't expecting to see you both here,' said Thomas.

'Well, after the fiasco at Blackfriars Abbey, the king has decided to go on a little tour of his realm to calm down,' said Stephen. 'I do not think he will stray too far from London. But he is restless and frustrated that it did not go his way at the hearing.'

'We have been farmed out to local gentry for food and board, while the king lodges at Waltham Abbey.' said Edward.

'Can you tell me what happened at Blackfriars Abbey?' Thomas asked.

Edward shifted in his seat and moved in closer to his colleagues. 'The pope appointed Cardinal Campeggio to oversee the king's appeal for an annulment of his marriage, at Blackfriars Abbey a couple of weeks ago. The king was putting pressure on the cardinal for a quick decision regarding his divorce,' said Edward.

'However,' interrupted Stephen, 'it turns out that Campeggio had secret orders from Rome to slow things down. Instead of deciding in the king's favour, and annulling the king's marriage to the queen, he stalled the proceedings by delaying the matter until October!'

'The king is livid,' said Edward, 'and so was Charles Brandon, the Duke of Suffolk. He thumped the table with his fist and yelled, "There never was a cardinal that did good for England!"'

'Yes, well, Suffolk and the king are good friends,' said Stephen.

'Catherine has been demanding that the pope hears the case in Rome. She knows that he will never allow the marriage to be dissolved,' said Edward.

'Not to mention that Pope Clement is afraid of the Emperor, Charles,' added Stephen. 'It is common knowledge that the emperor is the nephew of Queen Catherine. The last thing the pope wants is to be on the wrong side of Charles's displeasure.'

'You can't blame him for that,' said Edward. 'Being the King of Spain and the Holy Roman Emperor makes Charles a very powerful man.'

'Yes, it does,' said Stephen seriously.

'The king is used to getting what he wants,' retorted Thomas. 'Did Cardinal Campeggio get out of Blackfriars with his head still attached to his shoulders?' he asked jokily. 'You remember what happened to the Duke of Buckinghamshire?'

'Poor Edward Stafford,' said Edward. 'He was a close companion of the king too. I think it took the axeman three attempts. Just awful.'

'I remember that day,' said Stephen, 'and I remember the sound, like chopping wood. Well, the king is not happy that the pope continues to refuse him.'

Thomas thought for a moment. The break in the conversation allowed the men to fill their goblets with some more wine. Dr Fox broke the silence.

'Thomas, what do you think about the king's Great Cause?' he inquired. 'The king has placed me in charge of the matter. And to be frank, it's been going on for two years now. The king grows ever more restless with Pope Clement. We have tried everything to get the pope to pronounce a verdict on the king's divorce, but we are stonewalled at every turn.'

'I haven't thought about it too much,' Thomas began, 'but I believe that the king is going about this in the wrong way.'

'Don't let him hear you say that!' exclaimed Stephen.

'I like my head just where it is, so I promise you I won't,' said Thomas, smiling wryly. 'In my opinion, going to the church courts in Rome will simply prolong the matter,' said Thomas. 'You will waste a lot of time and energy trying to get the decision you want. The question of whether a man should marry his brother's wife must be decided by the Word of God. The Scriptures will show the truth about it. And in my view, there are none better to pronounce a verdict on the king's divorce than the theologians of the universities of England and Europe.'

Edward looked at Stephen and grinned. Then he turned to Thomas and exclaimed, 'Dr Cranmer, I do declare that you are a sage! May we let the king know of your counsel, perhaps he will go for it?' asked Edward.

'I doubt I have said anything that has not been thought of before,' said Thomas, 'but if you feel it will help, by all means tell the king.'

The two men were able to hide from Thomas just how desperate they were for a solution to the king's problem. They were willing to entertain any suggestion that had a modicum of sense about it. They would pitch this idea to King Henry and make sure he knew it came from Dr Cranmer. If the king hated it, then he would rent his anger on Thomas. But if he liked it, Fox and Gardiner will have done well in bringing such a good suggestion to the ear of the king.

The next day, Edward and Stephen left for the king's procession, leaving Thomas at Waltham. It wasn't until the day after that, that they had an audience with King Henry. Gardiner and Fox told the king enthusiastically of Thomas Cranmer's suggestion to seek counsel from the king's theologians in England. All the while, they watched the monarch's reaction. Would he like the idea, or loathe it? It was hard to tell with the king. He usually got what he wanted. But when he did not get his own way, he could become irascible and unpredictable.

When the two scholars had finished relaying the gist of the dinner conversation to their sovereign, the king appeared elated with their news. 'Indeed,' he said to them, 'I will speak with Dr Cranmer immediately. I see that that man has the sow by the right ear,' meaning that as far as the king was concerned, Thomas understood his situation perfectly. Thomas didn't really want to get involved with the matter of the king's divorce. There were other men just as capable as he, working tirelessly for a solution. But no one in England refused their king, especially a lowly professor of divinity from a Cambridge university.

Thomas met King Henry in the autumn of 1529 at Greenwich Palace, an opulent bastion built on the bank of the River Thames that flows through London. The king gave him the responsibility of writing down his ideas. His work would be used to argue on behalf of the king in his bid to rid himself of his wife, Catherine of Aragon. The king arranged for Dr Cranmer to stay with Thomas Boleyn, the Earl of Wiltshire, in the palatial surroundings of Durham House. Thomas would be comfortable there. And he would get plenty of peace and quiet to get on with the work in hand.

A Very Big Problem

The king's 'Great Cause', as it was known, became a very big problem for England, the Church and for Thomas Cranmer. Prince Henry was only seventeen when he came to the throne of England in 1509. Thomas was studying for a bachelor's degree at Jesus College in Cambridge at that time. Born on 2nd July 1489, Thomas was roughly two years older than King Henry, who was born on 28th June 1491. Thomas was blissfully unaware of the machinations of political life in the king's court, although he would not remain ignorant of them. Two decades later, Thomas would find himself in the king's service and an enthusiastic advocate for the king's divorce from Catherine.

The problem began with King Henry's engagement to Catherine of Aragon in September 1502. She was the wife of his older brother, Arthur who was the Prince of Wales. Prince Arthur married Catherine of Aragon in London on 14th November 1501. They were both very young. Arthur was only fifteen years old. Catherine was the seventeen-year-old daughter of King Ferdinand

and Queen Isabella of Spain. Their marriage brought a good and beneficial relationship between England and Spain. The young couple were only together for five months when Arthur got sick. He didn't get better and died on 2nd April 1502. Catherine was now widowed at the tender age of eighteen.

The Spanish Ambassador in England was instructed by his monarchs to begin negotiations with the English royalty concerning another marriage, this time between Catherine of Aragon and Prince Henry. The deliberations were successful. The pope issued a dispensation[1] that overruled church law and the teaching of Scripture prohibiting a man marrying his brother's wife[2]. Thus, the marriage was able to go ahead. Eventually the young couple were wed on 11th June 1509 in the church of the Franciscans at Greenwich, less than two months after Henry was crowned King of England, on 24th April 1509.

King Henry wanted a son to be heir to the throne in England. But the king and queen's efforts to produce one repeatedly failed. By the autumn of 1514, Queen Catherine had bore four children, three of them boys. But tragically none of them survived more than seven weeks. Their fifth baby, Mary, was born on 18th February 1516 and survived into adulthood. Queen

---

1. A dispensation gave the pope in Rome the right to excuse someone from obeying a particular church law or teaching of Scripture. It was sometimes called a papal dispensation.
2. 'If a man takes his brother's wife, it is impurity. He has uncovered his brother's nakedness; they shall be childless' (Leviticus 20:21 ESV).

Catherine became pregnant again in 1518, but tragedy struck one more time and the child was stillborn.

The lack of a male heir made Henry start to believe that perhaps God was angry with him for marrying his brother's wife. This thought festered in the king's mind. Then one day, after sharing his bed with her for eighteen years, Henry concluded that he and Catherine were never truly married. In 1527, the king requested that Pope Clement VII revoke the original dispensation which permitted the marriage in the first place. The pregnancy disasters persuaded him that he had committed a sin by marrying Catherine. Henry quoted Leviticus 20:21 as his reason for a divorce.

However not everyone agreed with Henry's understanding of the Scriptures on this matter. Most were just afraid to tell him. The Church did not take divorce lightly because it is God who joins a man and a woman together in holy matrimony and therefore it should not be torn apart by anyone. The Church may have granted a divorce for those who found themselves betrayed by their spouse. It might also have granted one for those whose partner was violent and abusive. But the reason that Henry gave for divorcing Catherine, would require a greater theological mind than his to persuade the pope to give him what he wanted.

The queen was horrified. As far as she was concerned, the marriage was fine and there was no way she would agree to a divorce from her husband. She thought they loved each other. And what would happen to Princess Mary? Catherine did not want to see Mary removed from the direct line of succession. King Henry, however, did not want to leave his kingdom to a daughter. Neither he, nor the rest of England, desired to risk a controversy over who would be heir to the throne in England. He wanted a son to rule the land when he was dead and gone.

There was another complication. Henry wasn't faithful to Catherine over the years. He had a mistress back in 1519, Elizabeth Blount, who gave birth to his son. They named him Henry Fitzroy. At the age of six, the king made him the first Duke of Richmond. It was an attempt to make the boy a plausible heir to the throne of England. Naturally this put a strain on the king's marriage to Catherine. However, they stayed together because there was still a possibility that Catherine would give him a son.

Then there was Mary Boleyn, the daughter of the Earl of Wiltshire and sister of Anne. She held the king's affections for a time. But when Henry saw Anne as she was tending to the needs of the queen, he discarded Mary like a dirty rag and directed his attention on to her sister. The king became infatuated with Anne and wanted her to be his wife. There was still the problem of his marriage to Catherine. Anne had made it clear that she would not encourage the king's advances while he was still married to the queen.

While all this was going on in Greenwich, Thomas Cranmer continued his peaceful existence as a

Cambridge academic in the gentle surroundings of Jesus College. It was home to him. He arrived there in 1503, the young man of lesser English gentry from Aslocton, east of Nottingham and not too far away from Sherwood Forest. He came from a large family. Thomas had two brothers and four sisters. His father was called Thomas and his mother was Agnes. His father sadly died in 1501, just before young Thomas turned twelve years old.

Thomas studied hard over the years. He had a habit of reading slowly and carefully, and he usually had a quill in his hand to jot down notes and comments in the margins of his books. His perseverance paid off as he got his Arts degree in 1511. Soon after, he was appointed a Fellow[3] of his college. From then on, Thomas devoted his life to studying theology[4]. He loved his Bible. And he admired the writings of Erasmus of Rotterdam[5]. Thomas was determined to attain further academic qualifications at Jesus College. He got his Master's in 1515, a Batchelor of Divinity degree in 1521 and by 1526 he was awarded his Doctor of Divinity.

Dr Cranmer was always ready to correct his colleagues if they were at fault in their academic arguments. He never allowed anyone to proceed in their education unless they were knowledgeable of Scripture. Many a monk or friar hated him for it. But

---

3. A *Fellow* is a senior lecturer in a university.

4. *Theology* is the study of God and religious belief.

5. *Erasmus* was a Dutch scholar who taught against dishonesty, injustice, and superstition in the church.

when they took his chastisement seriously and learned the Scriptures for themselves, they often praised good Dr Cranmer for helping them to see God's mercy and grace in the Word of God, the Bible.

Over time Thomas developed a good reputation among the universities of Cambridge. His academic prowess did not go unnoticed by Cardinal Wolsey, the Archbishop of York and King Henry's chief advisor. Thomas Wolsey was the most powerful man in England, after the king. He stood in for the king in day-to-day administration while Henry hunted and jousted. The cardinal became so powerful in the land that he had the nickname of *alter rex*, meaning the other king. Not too bad for the son of a butcher.

Cardinal Wolsey was always on the lookout for talented clergy to join his diplomatic team. At the beginning of 1527, Thomas was recruited to the king's service and played a small part in the English Embassy in Spain. It was important that the king knew what his Spanish counterpart, King Charles V, was doing in Europe. Relationships between nations always need hard work and diplomacy to avoid war. And Henry was known for liking war, especially with France.

Not only was Charles the King of Spain, but he was also the Holy Roman Emperor. He was bestowed this title in 1519, defeating the ruler of England who considered himself as a potential emperor. The Holy Roman Empire covered a vast area incorporating countries from western and central Europe.

Cranmer's role in Spain was minor and only for a short time. When he returned to England that summer, he was given a very warm reception. As a reward for his diplomatic work oversees, Thomas received an audience with the king himself. While the meeting was only for half an hour, it was long enough for King Henry to give him gifts of gold and silver rings for his service. This was the first meeting of the two men. Neither knew at that stage how much their lives would be entwined over the following years of Henry's reign.

Thomas knew of the king's desire for Anne Boleyn. Everyone knew, it was not a secret. Since her arrival at the king's court from her spell with the French royal family, Anne was seen as vivacious and mannerly. However enthusiasts for Queen Catherine spread a rumour that Anne was a witch due to her disfigured hand with an undeveloped sixth finger. This did nothing to quell the king's desire for Anne and the rumour was squashed.

Cardinal Wolsey was under orders from the king to persuade Pope Clement VII to annul Henry's marriage to Catherine of Aragon. He was uniquely placed to do this as the papal ambassador in England. He was the man with a direct line of communication to the pope. He could sway the pope to decide in favour of the king's appeal for a divorce. Persuading the pope would be a difficult task, especially as Cardinal Wolsey had sympathy for his queen. But he was loyal to his king and would do his duty.

The pope arranged for a hearing to commence at Blackfriars Abbey in the city of London on 28th May 1529. He appointed Cardinal Lorenzo Campeggio to oversee the court, not Wolsey. Nonetheless, Henry had the highest hopes for this court and was pressing for a quick decision. He was convinced that the cardinal would deliver a verdict in his favour and annul his marriage with Catherine. Instead, the king was frustrated in his bid to liberate himself from his wife. Cardinal Campeggio had secret orders from Rome to stall proceedings. On 30th July, he adjourned the hearing until October later that year. Catherine had been demanding that Pope Clement VII hear the case in Rome. Her nephew, Charles V of Spain, had backed her appeal. The delay to the arraignment would allow time for Catherine's appeal to reach the pope in Rome. But the pressure of it all drove the pope to his sickbed, and from there, he took back all the powers he had given the court at Blackfriars.

Wolsey had failed the king. Henry was infuriated. He lost patience with his papal legate. He stripped Cardinal Wolsey of his positions of power and packed him off to York to do the job of archbishop. In an attempt to win back the favour of his monarch, Wolsey gifted his palatial residence at Hampton Court to Henry. But it didn't work. He was out and would never regain his good standing with the King of England. A broken man, Wolsey retreated to York and died the following year, dejected, and disgraced.

Henry's plight had ground to a virtual standstill, that is, until the dinner in Waltham during the first week in August 1529. Perhaps that's why Dr Cranmer's idea was received at Greenwich Palace with such great enthusiasm. There was a way forward. The king needed someone to argue that the whole case of his existing marriage to Catherine of Aragon rested upon the priority of the Scriptures over the pope. It was ok for the papacy to disregard some of its own church laws, but it could not dispense from those of the Bible, the king thought.

The king had found his champion. He was called Thomas Cranmer, the quiet clergyman from Jesus College in Cambridge. Thomas would lead the king to victory over the papacy. No one tells the English Sovereign what he can and cannot do, not even the pope in Rome.

A Trip to Rome

It was January 1530 before Thomas could bring any of his research to the notice of the king. Henry liked to read everything first. It's not that Henry doubted Thomas's ability. After all he did think the world of Thomas. He would often say at court that Dr Cranmer was a wonderfully virtuous and wise man, whose advice had brought great help and comfort to him in his time of need.

'I hope it lasts,' said Mr Boleyn to Thomas. 'You know the king thought well of Wolsey. And look how that ended.'

'I know,' replied Thomas.

Mr Boleyn breathed in deeply the crisp morning air, as the two men walked through the beautifully landscaped garden at Durham House that led down to the banks of the River Thames. He stopped and turned to Thomas. 'I hope that your stay here has been comfortable, Dr Cranmer,' said Mr Boleyn. 'It has been a great privilege to have you. My daughters, Mary and Anne, have greatly benefited from your conversations with them about the Bible.' He started to walk again. 'According to Anne, you say the good news of Christ proclaims that anyone can be right with God?'

'Yes, anyone,' replied Thomas.

'Are not some more deserving of God's love than others, especially if they do many good things?' asked Mr Boleyn.

'None of us are deserving, Mr Boleyn. The Bible says that our sins make us spiritually dead. And we know that dead things cannot make themselves alive.'

'True indeed' said Mr Boleyn, thoughtfully. Thomas smiled and carried on.

'We need God to breathe new life into us. Therefore, salvation is his gift to us. It is not something that we can earn by ourselves. The Bible tells us that all our good works are like filthy rags if they are only done to please God and earn a place in heaven. That is why God's grace is so wonderful because it is offered to those who do not deserve it – which is all of us.'

'If we cannot earn God's salvation, Dr Cranmer, how do we receive this grace of God?'

'Well, it is only through Christ that we can know God's grace and kindness to us, especially his death on the cross and his resurrection from the grave. It is not a dead Christ we serve, Mr Boleyn, but a living Christ, isn't that right?'

'Thanks be to God!' exclaimed Mr Boleyn.

'We can only know Christ Jesus through the Scriptures, but here is the problem,' said Thomas.

'How do you mean, Dr Cranmer?' asked Mr Boleyn.

'It is my desire that everyone in the realm of England should be able to read the Bible for themselves. But alas, it is in the Latin tongue, and not many understand it. How I would love the Bible to be available in every church across the land in the common language of the people.'

'That is a grand dream, Dr Cranmer. Do not lose sight of it,' said Mr Boleyn.

'It is so important that the people should know Christ and put their trust in Him. My heart breaks for those who do not know Him, Mr Boleyn,' said Thomas. 'Trusting God should change our lives. Can you imagine what this country would be like if all put their faith in Christ alone?'

'It is too fanciful to imagine, my good Dr Cranmer,' said Mr Boleyn.

'Perhaps,' replied Thomas. 'Nonetheless, whatever our number, those who serve Christ must do so in a manner that glorifies Christ, and not ourselves. There is too much false humility in the Church as it stands.'

The two men walked in silence to the bank of the River Thames. Mr Boleyn was mulling over the conversation when Thomas broke the silence. 'I am indebted to you and your wonderful family for such gracious hospitality, Mr Boleyn. I am only saddened that my time with you all has come to an end.'

'When do you leave for Cambridge?'

'Soon,' replied Thomas. 'His Majesty would like my work to be sent to my academic colleagues in

Cambridge. No doubt I shall be required to explain my findings to them as well. I hope that my presence will serve to enforce the argument for the king. There are still some who are not convinced of the king's position. Does the king have anything in mind for you, my lord?'

'His Majesty requires my services in Italy next month, to represent him at the coronation of the emperor Charles, in Bologna.'

'That will be a grand occasion,' said Thomas.

'It will, Thomas. And once you have spoken to your cohort in Cambridge, the king would like you to join my embassy. John Stokesley and Edward Lee will also be part of it.'

Thomas did not see that one coming.

'But your mission will be different to ours. We shall travel through France before we get to Italy. You are to do in the universities of France and Italy what you will do in Cambridge and Oxford. Persuade the divines of the king's cause. This will strengthen His Majesty's argument when it comes before the pope. Do you understand, Dr Cranmer?'

'Yes, I understand, my lord,' replied Thomas. 'There is no time to lose. I must leave for Cambridge post-haste.'

His trip to universities in Cambridge and Oxford proved successful. Thomas was able to win over many of his academic colleagues there who had been opposed to the king. Their favourable verdict was sent by Henry to his royal ambassadors. They would lay it before the pope.

The journey by boat across the English Channel to France was pleasantly uneventful. The weather was fair and the waters calm. The entourage made its way slowly through France. There was no hurry getting to Italy it seemed. They were looking forward to seeing some of the beautiful cities of France on their way to the coronation in Bologna. They visited the universities of Paris, Orleans, Anjou, Bourges, and Toulouse. Thomas set the king's Great Cause before them and won favourable replies in each university.

'Your arguments are very compelling, Dr Cranmer,' said Edward Lee. 'I can see why the king has chosen you to represent His Majesty in this matter.'

'We have done well to secure these votes in France. I hope that we can do as well in Italy,' replied Thomas.

'Come now, Dr Cranmer, do not be modest,' said Thomas Boleyn, the Earl of Wiltshire.

'A priest should always be humble, my lord,' replied Thomas.

'You should have told that to Cardinal Wolsey!' exclaimed Edward. 'At the height of his power, I believe he required his bishops to tie his shoes and dukes to hold his washbasin!'

The Royal Ambassadors continued to journey south-east into Italy and found the pope at the end of March in Bologna, having just crowned Charles V for the third time, as Holy Roman Emperor. The pope had no intention of causing the emperor any offence. The trip made by the Royal Representatives appeared futile, so much so that Thomas Boleyn and Edward Lee retraced their steps through France in the early summer while John Stokesley stayed in Bologna. Thomas, however, journeyed to the beautiful northern city of Venice. On his way, he persuaded three more Italian universities to pronounce in favour of the king. He was making good progress, but he had still to persuade the pope to grant the annulment.

Thomas finally arrived in Rome in the summer of 1530. He was met by the English Ambassador in Rome, Jerome Ghinucci, who was also the Bishop of Worcester. Thomas and Jerome had met in Spain back in 1527, when they were representing the king's interests there. Jerome was happy to see Thomas. Defending the king's position in Rome was proving to be a difficult task, and he was glad to have someone to share the load. Thomas made an offer to debate the king's issue before the pope, but his offer was not welcomed. Even the positive votes from the Cambridge and Oxford universities that were sent to Rome to be laid before the pope didn't change his mind. The pope and his cardinals were very much against the English ambassadors in their midst. Thomas felt a sense of gloom. There was nothing he could do or say that would change the pope's view of Henry's cause.

At the bishop's residence on a warm August evening in Rome, the two clerics reflected on their progress so far over dinner. 'The pope is obstinate,' said Jerome. 'I have been representing His Majesty's interests here for a while, but there seems to be nothing I can say to get Clement to change his mind.'

'I am experiencing the same thing,' Thomas said glumly.

'Well, misery loves company, Dr Cranmer,' laughed Jerome. Thomas smiled. When his laughter died down, the bishop looked seriously at Thomas. 'I have something that may cheer you up,' he said quietly.

'It would be a most welcome distraction, Bishop,' replied Thomas.

'My position as Bishop of Worcester comes with a number of privileges,' began the bishop. 'It is within my power to gift parishes within my diocese back in England, Thomas, and I think I have just the one for you.'

Thomas listened intently as the bishop continued. 'There is a fine parish in Bredon, Thomas. There are good people there and you will not have to worry about money. It's a wealthy place. I would like to make you the rector[1] of Bredon, Thomas. What do you think about that?'

Thomas was overwhelmed by the bishop's generosity to him, a lowly college professor. 'I do not know what to say, Bishop, only thank you,' he replied.

'You have earned it, Thomas.'

There was no doubt in Cranmer's mind that he had worked very hard for the king's cause. Although

---

1. A *rector* is the title given to a priest in charge of a church.

he wasn't seeking promotion, it was nice to have his efforts recognised. Yet no matter how hard he tried he could not overcome the hostility he felt from the pope's legates. So, he left Rome in September and returned to England, picking up Stokesley in Bologna on the way. They arrived at the port in Calais and boarded the ship destined for England. Thomas was looking forward to getting back to his precious college in Cambridge and the peaceful life that it gave him. And it wasn't as hot in the summer months in Cambridge. Rome's heat was unbearable to a man that was used to cooler climates.

Stokesley and Cranmer arrived in England in the middle of October 1530. Their mission for the king was over and it was time to get back to life as normal, or so he thought. Cranmer was pleased that he did not disgrace himself on the Continent. In fact, he did quite well, securing the votes of seven universities in France and Italy. He was sure that the king would be happy with his efforts. Indeed, the king was contented with him, but instead of allowing Thomas to return to his academic life at Jesus College, Henry instructed the Rector of Bredon to explore further all the complexities of his Great Cause. The king did not want the papacy to find any excuse to refuse him. He was Sovereign in the realm of England, not Pope Clement VII. And there was the crux of the matter. Who held the power in England?

So, the king attempted to intimidate the English clergy into rejecting papal authority and accepting him as the head of both the church and state. Thwarted by the pope who refused to annul his marriage to Catherine of Aragon, Henry determined to settle the matter at home by making the clergy bend to his will. When the convocations[2] of York and Canterbury met, he shocked the bishops by announcing that they and their clergy, were all guilty of *praemunire*. It was an old law that was devised to safeguard against excessive foreign influence in England. Henry accused the clergy of treason, by claiming royal authority for themselves and accepting the influence of Rome in matters of religion. This was a very serious offence which was punishable by imprisonment and loss of all assets to the king. However, the monarch would pardon all of them if they paid a fine of £100,000 and recognised him as 'Protector and only Supreme Head of the Church and Clergy of England.'

It was strange that the king was condemning his clergy. It was their duty to obey church authority. They vowed to do so at their ordination. And up to this point, the king had been loyal to the authority of the church as well.

Lengthy discussions followed and the clergy decided that they would submit to the king with the caution that Henry was supreme head of the Church only 'as far as the law of Christ allows.' Thomas agreed with this. He was not a fan of the papacy. He had always felt that the king should be the supreme head of the Church of

---

2. A *convocation* is an assembly of bishops and other clergy.

England and not the papacy. But King Henry VIII was not greater than the Lord Jesus Christ, the King of Kings. Thomas was confident that even the monarch of England agreed with that assertion.

In the King's Service

The Reformation in Europe had a champion. Martin Luther emerged as a critic of the Roman Catholic Church in Germany in 1517. He could see that the Church had drifted away from the Bible and had elevated man-made traditions and practices that had no basis in the Scriptures. He posted a list of 95 theses on a church door at Wittenberg. Criticising the church for its use of indulgences[1] he argued that priests should not stand between men and the teachings of the Bible. Luther's challenge to the established church was followed by a denial of transubstantiation – the teaching that says at the moment of blessing performed by the priest, the bread and wine of the Mass[2] become the actual body and blood of Christ.

As a nation, England was staunchly Roman Catholic during the early part of the sixteenth century. King

---

1. *Indulgences* were sold for money as pardons from purgatory – the place where souls were thought to suffer after death to work off some of the punishment for their sins.
2. *The Mass* is the name given by Roman Catholics to the Lord's Supper, or Holy Communion.

Henry VIII came to the throne in 1509 and was a devout young man. At one point he thought about becoming a priest in the church. He studied theology before the death of his older brother, Arthur, made him the heir to the throne of England.

The shocking news of Luther's rebellion against the church in Germany crossed the channel to England. Henry opposed Luther's views and became known as the Defender of the Faith, a title that is still held by the English monarch today. Luther's teachings were gaining significant ground in England by 1525. There were many students and academic professors in Cambridge, who liked to meet in the local taverns and discuss Luther's views about the Church, the Lord's Supper, and the Bible.

Thomas Cranmer never supported a new idea quickly. He read everything slowly and he always had a quill pen in his hand to make notes in the margins of the pages. He thought long and hard about an issue before accepting any truth that was new to him. Perhaps this was a reason why the Reformation in England began slowly. Thomas was not willing to accept Luther's view about the Mass until he had studied the Scriptures and the writings of the early Church Fathers. He wasn't about to jump on the Reformation bandwagon. On the other hand, Luther was not willing to support Cranmer's argument for an annulment of the king's marriage to Catherine of Aragon. Luther had sympathy for Catherine and a great dislike for divorce.

By 1531, Dr Cranmer's views as a priest of the church in England were not much different from his clergy colleagues. However, there were some things that he did not agree with. Thomas believed that it was right for the sovereign of England to be the supreme head of the church in his own realm, not the pope in Rome. Thomas disdained the pope, almost as much as King Henry. It is true that the king disliked anyone trying to usurp his authority as the monarch of England. If they were a subject of his kingdom, then it was treason, punishable by death, usually in the form of beheading. And Thomas also thought that clergy ought to marry if they wanted to. He kept that view close to his chest, at least for the time being.

It wasn't until the end of the year that Thomas formally entered the service of the King of England. He was invited to be a chaplain. It was a great honour for any cleric and of course, one that could not be refused. Seriously, it was a bad idea to refuse the King of England. Thankfully, Thomas saw it as an opportunity to offer spiritual guidance and pastoral care to the king whenever he needed it. He thought that he could help influence Henry for the good of the nation. He wasn't aware just how much good he would do for England in the future. He was simply the king's servant.

Around the same time, his colleague Dr Gardiner had been rewarded for his service to the monarch. He became the Bishop of Worcester, taking over from Cranmer's friend from the Spanish mission, Jerome

Ghinucci. It meant that there was a vacancy in the post of Archdeacon of Taunton, a position that Dr Gardiner held. This was offered to Thomas, who gladly accepted the role. A chaplain to the king and the Archdeacon of Taunton. 'What next?' he wondered.

He didn't have to wait too long before he found that out. King Henry had already told the Holy Roman Emperor, Charles V, of his new theological champion. The king was giving his opponent the opportunity to scrutinise Dr Cranmer for himself, as he was sending the good Doctor to be a royal ambassador in the Imperial Court of the Emperor. What Henry didn't tell Charles, was that he was giving his ambassador secret orders to contact the German Protestants to see if there was any possibility of an alliance with England against the Empire. Henry wasn't getting anywhere with Rome concerning his Great Cause. He was now looking for support from churches that had splintered their connections with the Holy Roman Empire, to see if they could help him.

The Archdeacon of Taunton was dispatched to the Court of Charles V in Germany during the early months of 1532. Thomas spent time with the Emperor in his Imperial Court in Ratisbon, south-east Germany. As the Emperor was the nephew of Catherine of Aragon, Thomas was sure that he would not be able to obtain Charles's support for the king's divorce. His mission wasn't a complete waste of time, however. He did gain a lot of diplomatic experience in the process.

Then in July, Thomas slipped away to meet some of the German Protestants in the large city of Nuremburg, not far from the Imperial base of Ratisbon. The city leaders of Nuremberg had shown support for Martin Luther's reformation. It was here that Thomas developed a firm friendship with a local preacher called Andreas Osiander. Thomas discovered that his new friend had a love for the Scriptures and was writing a book about the Gospels. This was very exciting as far as Thomas was concerned. He loved the Bible too and he was earnest to learn more of Andreas's book.

Early in the morning of a beautiful spring day in Nuremberg, Thomas made the trek from his lodgings to the home of his new friend. He walked past the castle in the centre of the city. It was a strong fortification, built centuries earlier and used by German kings and Holy Roman Emperors who travelled to the city. Thomas thought it was an impressive building. It gave the impression that its residents were people of power and affluence.

Thomas soon arrived at the more modest home of Andreas Osiander. He thumped the door hard a few times with his clenched fist. He was confident that Andreas was up out of his bed and would welcome him gladly.

The door creaked open, to reveal the bearded face of the pastor of St Lorenz. 'Dr Cranmer, what a wonderful surprise,' said Andreas. 'Please come in.'

'I hope you do not mind my visit this morning, Andreas,' said Thomas as he entered.

'Not at all,' replied his friend. 'I am so glad that you are here. This is my wife, Katharina,' he said, motioning to an elegant lady walking from the compact kitchen next to the sitting room.

'It is my pleasure to meet you, Mrs Osiander,' said Thomas, bowing his head. She smiled at Thomas. It was clear to him that perhaps her English wasn't as good as her husband's.

As Thomas walked to an empty chair next to a small fire burning in the grate, he noticed a desk covered with paper. 'It looks like you are very busy, Andreas,' said Thomas, pointing to the unfinished work sitting on the desk. 'If I am disturbing you, I can call another day.'

'You are not disturbing me, Dr Cranmer. Please sit and stay a while,' replied Andreas. 'I have been working on a book for some time now. Presently I am finding it hard to write anything further.'

'What are you writing about?' asked Thomas.

'It is a book about the Gospels of Jesus. I want to show how the story of Christ in each Gospel can be drawn together to give a clear and full picture of his life.'

'This will be a very helpful book indeed!' exclaimed Thomas.

'It will be if I can finish it,' said Andreas.

'You must!' declared Thomas. 'Perhaps I can help get you unstuck.'

Andreas looked at Cranmer willingly. Thomas pulled his chair next to the desk. 'Come and sit,' he said pointing to another chair by the table. 'Let us discuss the Gospels of our Lord and Saviour,' he said.

Andreas smiled and walked quickly to the table. Sitting side by side, the two men talked for ages about Jesus Christ. As the conversation progressed, Andreas was beginning to think of ways that he could write more. He was so grateful to Thomas for his time and encouragement. He was concentrating so much that he didn't hear the knock on the door. Katharina opened it to reveal a beautiful young lady standing in the doorway.

Andreas turned to see Katharina's niece standing in the room, looking bewildered by the animated conversation at her uncle's writing desk. He stood and greeted her warmly. Then without further ado, he introduced her to his new friend, Thomas Cranmer.

Thomas stood clumsily knocking over his chair. He looked at her and bowed his head. 'Hello, Margarete,' he said. He could feel his face getting redder with embarrassment.

Margarete giggled and greeted him in German. '*Guten tag*, Herr Cranmer,' she said. Osiander's niece did not know any English, but that did not matter to Thomas. She was the picture of loveliness in his eyes.

Cranmer cleared his throat and said, 'My dear Andreas. I had not realised the time passing. I must go now. But perhaps I can call again someday?' he asked.

'Yes, yes of course!' exclaimed Andreas, 'our conversation has been truly inspirational. You can call with me whenever you want.'

Thomas bade the ladies farewell and departed quickly. He had not expected such an interesting morning. He found the discussion with Andreas stimulating. There was nothing better than talking about the Bible. Thomas loved every minute of it. The other surprise was meeting his host's niece. She seemed like a sweet girl, and he hoped that he would meet Margarete again, although he did not know how they would get to know each other, as neither spoke the other's language. However, where there's a will, there's a way. Perhaps he could rely on Andreas to help break down the communication barrier with Margarete.

There was a lightness in his step that afternoon as he returned to his lodgings. Could it be true, love at first sight was really possible? But his fantasy came crashing down as he remembered that he was a priest in the Church. He had taken a vow at his ordination to remain celibate. Not only that, but he was also a royal ambassador on the king's business at the Imperial Court of the Holy Roman Emperor.

'It would be madness to risk my life over a girl,' Thomas murmured to himself. 'The king would take a very dim view of such rebellion from a trusted servant.' He walked in silence a bit further. Then he stopped in his tracks. 'I hope she is there on my next visit!' he boldly said and laughed.

The Promotion

It was a beautiful day for a wedding. There were no clouds in the sky. The sun was shining. The air was warm and still. The birds were singing melodiously perched high up on the church's two towers. Thomas was happy. But as he walked closer to the church building in Nuremberg, he could feel a knot forming in the pit of his stomach. It was right for him to feel nervous on his wedding day. 'Till death do us part,' he said to himself. 'That could be a long time.'

Over breakfast that morning, Thomas thought of the first time he got married, back in 1516. It was the year after he received his Master's degree from Jesus College. He was working as a professor of divinity there. She was a lovely girl called Joan. He met her at the Dolphin Inn, at the end of All Saint's Lane in Cambridge. The men from Jesus College used to meet there to socialise and relax after a hard day's work. Joan was a niece of the mistress of the Inn. It wasn't long before they fell in love and wanted to be together in matrimony. Thomas had to resign his position at Jesus

College, so that he could marry her. Fortunately, he was able to get another teaching position in the recently formed Magdalen College in Cambridge.

Joan and Thomas thought they would be together forever. He remembered the day when she told him they were expecting the pitter patter of tiny Cranmer feet in a few months. That was one of the happiest days of his life. Everything appeared to be going well, that is, until the day the baby was born. Sadly, there were bad difficulties and both Joan and the baby passed away. That was the worse day of his life. Thomas never got over it. His heart was broken. No human words could comfort him. In that time of deepest grief, he turned to the Bible and called out to the Lord to help him.

He recalled some words in the first chapter of a small New Testament letter called Colossians where the apostle Paul wrote to the church there: 'May you be strengthened with all power, according to his glorious might, for all endurance and patience with joy, giving thanks to the Father, who has qualified you to share in the inheritance of the saints in light. He has delivered us from the domain of darkness and transferred us to the kingdom of his beloved Son, in whom we have redemption, the forgiveness of sins.'[1]

Power. Everyone wants it. Everyone loves it. But Thomas felt so powerless. He felt weak and helpless in the face of death, in the midst of sorrow. Thomas knew the power of God at work in him over the years,

---

1. Colossians 1:11-14 RSV.

transforming his mind with the Word of God and helping him to live a life that was worthy of his calling as a servant of Jesus Christ. But what surprised him was what the apostle Paul said the power of God was for – to endure patiently and with joy and thanksgiving.

'I suppose we never need to endure in happy times,' Thomas thought. 'We never need patience when things are fun. We only need patience in bad or difficult times.' Thomas began to understand that the power of God was at work in every Christian, giving the endurance and the patience that is needed to deal with all the bad things in this difficult life. But to do it joyfully and with thanksgiving? Now, that was hard, even impossible. Did God really want him to be thankful for the death of his family? Of course not! He read the verses again and thought for a moment. The joy and the thanksgiving are linked to the inheritance that every believer has laid up in heaven. 'We have hope beyond this life,' Thomas said to himself, clutching his Bible close to his chest, as tears ran silently down his cheeks.

Soon after, Thomas was given the opportunity to teach once again at his beloved Jesus College in Cambridge and resumed his position as a professor of divinity. He threw himself into his work and his students' wellbeing to keep his mind occupied.

Sixteen years later, he was about to embark on another marital adventure with Margarete at his side. However, there was danger attached to this marriage unlike his first one. Now he was an ordained priest of the Church in England, who had vowed to be single the rest of his life, although for a long time he thought that there was no justification in the Bible for such a view. He was also a royal ambassador of King Henry VIII in the Imperial Court of the Holy Roman Emperor. If those men discovered that he was married, he could be in serious bother with the king and the Church. He determined that they had better not find out.

The church door creaked open to reveal a spacious building with a long aisle. Thomas could see the small figure of Andreas Osiander standing at the front of the church. Margarete had not yet arrived.

'Good morning, my dear friend,' said Andreas, hand stretched out to welcome the groom. Thomas took his hand, and they shook vigorously. 'What a beautiful day the Lord has provided for you to marry on,' he said enthusiastically.

'Good morning, Andreas. It is a lovely day,' replied Thomas. He looked down the church at the small number of guests in the pews. It was to be kept low key, so the couple did not invite too many to join in their celebrations. 'It's nearly time. She will be here?' asked Thomas nervously.

Andreas laughed and said, 'Yes of course she will. Do not worry. In fact…' He motioned with his head to the door. Thomas turned and saw his beautiful bride enter. He breathed a sigh of relief and beamed as she made her way to his side. She smiled sweetly at him. Her uncle began the ceremony that would unite Thomas and

Margarete as husband and wife. The ceremony seemed to happen very quickly as far as Thomas was concerned. That's a common feeling among newly-weds. Then it was time for some feasting at the home of Andreas and Katharina Osiander. There was much joy and laughter that afternoon. Thomas thanked the Lord for giving him a good wife. He prayed that he would be a good husband to Margarete. Sure, it was going to be hard for the new couple to be together, given the circumstances of Thomas's role in England and their lack of knowledge of each other's language. But they were confident that God would provide a way.

During this time, back in England, the convocations of Canterbury and York were put under pressure from the king and his parliament, to accept that Henry VIII, rather than the pope, had final authority over the English Church. There were some church leaders who struggled with this outcome. Those loyal to the papacy found it nigh impossible to move forward in their service of the king and resigned their positions. Others like Dr Cranmer and Dr Gardiner had little respect for the papacy while the pope continued to obstruct their royal master's wishes regarding his divorce.

Then came the shocking news of the death of the Archbishop of Canterbury, William Warham in a country house near Canterbury, just a month after the marriage of Thomas and Margarete in Germany. Now there was a vacancy in the most important and influential position of the Church of England. No doubt, there were some clergy who fancied the role, wondering if the king would reward them for their faithful service to the Crown. But Thomas was not thinking about it. He was settling into his job as the king's man in the Imperial Court. He also felt that being away from England gave him and Margarete the opportunity to solidify their marriage in secret and without threat.

The summons came during October 1532, while Thomas was in the Italian city of Mantua, with Charles V and his entourage. Thomas was amazed that he should receive such a call from England. He knew that the archbishop passed away during the summer, but he had no idea that his name was top of the list for replacing him. He thought either John Stokesley or Stephen Gardiner were obvious candidates to be the next Archbishop of Canterbury. Perhaps they thought the same. Thomas was sure they would not be happy at such a preferment levelled upon him by King Henry. He was unhappy that his new post would require him to be inducted by the pope. He was also troubled by the oath of obedience to papal authority which was required of him before his consecration[2] as archbishop. Surely this would mean a conflict with the duty that he owed to the Crown.

Yet there was something more immediate for Thomas to worry about. He had recently launched out into the unchartered and dangerous waters of clerical

---

2. This is a church ceremony that sets someone apart for a sacred office, such as an Archbishop or Bishop.

matrimony. What would Mrs Cranmer think of it all? He couldn't introduce her to the king, that would be madness. Rather than being greeted by the king's hand of welcome, he could be greeted by the executioner's axe of death! He thought long and hard about their future arrangements. He was aware that there were certain benefits that came with the position of Archbishop of Canterbury. There were properties at the primate's disposal, that could house a clandestine wife. Maybe Mrs Cranmer could stay at one of these and keep a low profile there? He would work something out.

There is not a doubt, it was an unpleasant surprise to Thomas that he should be required by his monarch to take up the highest position in the English Church. He was most unwilling to accept the promotion, but he saw it as his duty to comply with the king's wishes. Nonetheless, Thomas would not hurry back. He decided that he would prolong his journey to London, thinking that if he took his time travelling home, perhaps the king would forget about him, and appoint someone else. But the king did not forget about Dr Cranmer. Henry believed that the Archdeacon of Taunton was a man who was loyal, dependable, intelligent and good – just the sort of chap that would accept the king's supremacy of the church. Yes, he could use a good man like that. There would be no delay in the consecration of the new Archbishop of Canterbury.

Dr Cranmer did not land back in England until January 1533, but the king had already asked the pope for an official order declaring the nomination of Thomas Cranmer to be the new Archbishop of Canterbury. This came without delay and on 30th March 1533, in St Stephen's College in the Palace of Westminster, Thomas Cranmer was made the new Archbishop of Canterbury.

It was a day full of pomp and circumstance, as state affairs usually are. Inwardly Thomas was certain that his new position would not be easy. Every archbishop that preceded him had found it so because all the power to effect change, whether good or bad, lay in the hands of the king. Thomas and Henry could agree about the papacy, but what if Thomas should desire the reform of the English Church to a more Protestant position? His time in Europe with the Lutheran Princes made a positive impact on him. His conversations with his friend Andreas helped him to check every new idea against the Scriptures. Thomas would need his wits about him to navigate the affairs of the State and survive the rule of his impetuous master. His high office would bring inevitable dangers and conflicts. There were stormy years ahead of him. However, Thomas knew that under God he could use his new position to bring about a transformation in the churches of the land that would bring glory and honour to Christ in England. By the grace of God, he would do it.

The Ultimatum

The storm burst at once in the life of the new
Archbishop of Canterbury.

'The king has wasted no time in requesting that
I settle the matter for him,' said Thomas to his wife,
as they sat by the glowing fire in a small sitting room
of Lambeth Palace, the Archbishop of Canterbury's
London residence. Although Margarete only spoke
German and Thomas only English, they usually got
the gist of what the other was saying.

'What will you do?' asked Margarete.

'I shall open court in Dunstable Priory,' replied
Thomas.

'Where is that?'

'It's in Bedfordshire,' said Thomas, 'about fifty miles
north of London.'

'When do you start?' she enquired.

'In all likelihood, sometime in May,' said Thomas. 'I
will need to work out details with His Majesty.'

'I feel sorry for his poor wife,' said Margarete 'how
many years have they been together?'

'Twenty-six years,' answered Thomas.

'Twenty-six years,' she repeated. 'Such a pity.'

'It is a mess,' sighed Thomas. Of course, he could never say that in anyone's company other than Margarete, whom he trusted implicitly. Such thoughts must be kept private, especially in the king's presence.

Sometimes Thomas understated things to his wife. It was part of his thoughtful and level-headed nature. He was known for it. By now he was aware that the king had tested the church leadership towards the end of the previous year, to determine if they backed his desire for a divorce from Catherine of Aragon. With some reservation, they did. Therefore, Henry jumped the gun and married Anne Boleyn in a small and secret ceremony at the beginning of 1533. Even as the Archbishop of Canterbury, Thomas was not always privy to the exact details of the king's life. He didn't find out about the clandestine marriage until roughly a fortnight later. Soon after, Anne discovered that she was pregnant. The elated Henry hoped it was a boy.

Archbishop Cranmer opened court in Dunstable Priory on 10th May, 1533. An invitation had been extended to Queen Catherine, but she declined to attend. It was her opinion that Archbishop Cranmer did not have any right to try the case. From now on, spiritual matters would be decided in the king's courts and not in the courts of the papacy. On 23rd May, Archbishop Cranmer declared that the king's marriage to Catherine of Aragon was null and void from the outset, on the grounds that the pope did not possess the powers to overrule the Scriptures.

The following week, Thomas had the onerous duty of endorsing the marriage of King Henry VIII to Anne Boleyn, even though he didn't officiate at it, nor did he know the exact date of the wedding. And now, the next thing that Thomas had to attend to, was the new queen's coronation[1]. The king was keen to make this a spectacle of royal magnificence as would prove irresistible to the people of London. Queen Anne was paraded through the city with a richly adorned company of lords, knights, and other important citizens of the realm. The Lord Mayor presented the queen with a gold cloth purse containing a thousand gold marks[2].

The onlookers who lined the streets of London were noticeably subdued. Anne's pregnancy was clear for all to see. Everyone knew that at the start of the year, when Anne told the king that she was pregnant, he was still wed to Catherine of Aragon. Citizens had only learned of the royal marriage three days ago. It was a lot to take in. The people had known Catherine of Aragon as Queen of England for twenty-four years and liked her, but they did not like Anne Boleyn so much.

The coronation took place at Westminster Abbey in the heart of London. Since 1066, the Abbey was the setting for every royal coronation. It was a grand

---

1. A *coronation* is an official ceremony of crowning a new monarch.
2. A *gold mark* was the unit of currency at the time, worth about £1.60 today.

occasion, full of pomp and circumstance. During the ceremony, Archbishop Cranmer, regaled in fine clerical robes and mitre, anointed Anne and placed the royal crown on her head. It was done. Anne Boleyn was the new Queen of England.

The banquet afterwards in the great hall was opulent, consisting of the finest food and drink that money could buy. The king spared no expense. There was much music and merriment.

Thomas sat quietly enjoying the feast before him. As he ate, he began to reflect on his first two weeks in the highest ecclesiastical office of the land. He concluded that recent events would not sit well with Pope Clement VII. Although the pope had given formal confirmation to his appointment as Archbishop of Canterbury, Thomas knew Clement would be angry with him for rejecting papal authority and for giving the king an annulment of his marriage to Catherine.

The following month, the king sent a delegation to Catherine with the task of getting her to surrender her title as queen and agree to be known as Princess Dowager of Wales. The title of Dowager was normally given to a widow of a monarch or nobility. She was given this new title in recognition of her position as Prince Arthur's widow. She was placed under house arrest at the Palace of Buckden in Cambridgeshire, with a substantial staff to cater for her needs. Her daughter Mary was removed from the line of succession to the throne of England. This would prove to be very problematic for the nation and for Archbishop Cranmer in the future. Although Catherine wanted Mary to stay with her in Buckden Palace, she was denied her wish. The new queen, Anne, did not allow Mary to see her parents. Instead, she stripped Mary of the title of princess and made her a lady-in-waiting for her new baby, Elizabeth. And although Mary did not see her mother again, she would never forget her.

When news of Archbishop Cranmer's apparent disloyalty reached Rome, the pope was outraged. And less than two weeks after the coronation of Anne Boleyn, Clement told Henry that he would be expelled from the Church if he refused to take back his discarded queen, Catherine. The king responded to the threat by recalling his ambassadors and triggering an Act of Parliament known as the 'Restraint of Annates' which severed all church payments made to Rome.

At Hampton Court Palace the king's new residence, the monarch and his archbishop walked in the beautifully fragrant rose garden and discussed the situation with Rome thus far. 'It is remarkable how people relent when you threaten to withhold money from them, my dear Archbishop,' said the king.

'Yes, Your Majesty,' replied Thomas. 'As the apostle Paul writes to Timothy in his first letter, the love of money is a root of all kinds of evil'.[3]

---

3. 1 Timothy 6:10.

'Indeed, Archbishop, indeed! It is certainly true that the papacy loves money,' retorted the king. 'All the money we have sent to Rome in the past, and for what?! An obstinate pope and a spineless cardinal.' The king was referring to Cardinal Thomas Wolsey who had been at Henry's side from the first days of his reign. Both Henry and Thomas knew that there was little popular opposition to their defiance of Rome.

As the autumn approached, there was much anticipation for the birth of the new baby in the royal household. Along with Henry's break from Rome, the royal baby was a favourite topic of conversation in the local taverns the length and breadth of England. Everyone was praying that the child would be a boy, for Anne's sake. On Sunday, 7th September between three and four in the afternoon, the wait was over. The queen gave birth to a beautiful healthy girl in Greenwich Palace. The king was relieved that mother and baby were well. And for now, he would hide his disappointment that a male heir was not born.

The king and queen asked Thomas to be the baby's godfather[4]. He was overjoyed and humbled at the invitation, that the rulers of England should trust him with such an important role in their family. Of course, he agreed the moment he was asked. At her baptism

---

4. A godfather is a man who makes promises to encourage his godchild to grow in the Christian faith and who commits to helping the child understand how to live a life in a way that pleases the Lord Jesus Christ.

on 10th September, 1533 at the Church of Observant Friars in Greenwich the king and queen named the princess, Elizabeth. Such a beautiful name for such a beautiful girl, thought Thomas. The Bishop of London, John Stokesley took her in his arms and baptised her in the name of God: Father, Son and Holy Spirit.

Suddenly there was a loud cry from the king's chief advisor. 'God of his infinite goodness, give a long and prosperous life to the high and mighty Princess of England, Elizabeth!' There was then a blast of trumpets that heralded the arrival of the new princess and deafened the congregation. Seventeen-year-old Princess Mary looked on in quiet displeasure, as now there was a rival for the throne of England. She just hoped that Anne wouldn't give him a son in the future.

That evening, in the quiet of his bedroom chamber, Thomas knelt to pray at his bedside as he did every night. He prayed in earnest that the new princess would never be ashamed to declare the faith of Christ crucified. He prayed that she would fight bravely against sin, the world, and the devil. He prayed that she would continue as a faithful soldier and servant of Christ to the very end of her life. God did finally use Elizabeth's life and reign for his own glory but sadly Thomas would not be around to see her become Queen of England.

Autumn turned to winter and with the king's blessing, Archbishop Cranmer embarked on a series of visitations, first around the Diocese of Canterbury and then around the Province of Canterbury[5], much to the annoyance of some of his bishops and clergy. Bishops Gardiner and Stokesley complained that it was unnecessary. But they were jealous of Cranmer. He had been gifted the highest ecclesiastical office in England, instead of one of them. And now to add insult to injury, here he comes, the big boss, checking up on them! They were suspicious of him. Actually, they were suspicious of everybody. But they really did not like it when the archbishop instructed all his clergy not to say anything anymore about certain unbiblical teachings of the Roman Catholic Church down through the ages, such as Masses for the dead, prayers to the saints, pilgrimages, and clerical celibacy (Thomas had abandoned that one a long time ago!).

What made the conservatives, like Gardiner and Stokesley furious, was Cranmer's appeal to convocation for a translation of the Scriptures in the English language. His vision was to have a copy of the Bible available in every church in the land. He prayed that God would grant him the strength, endurance and patience to see it come to pass in his beloved Church of England.

---

5. The **Province of Canterbury** is a large region roughly the size of two thirds of England. It contains approximately thirty Dioceses. A **Diocese** is a smaller area with churches and other clergy, over which a bishop has authority.

The Queen's Advocate

The Archbishop of Canterbury fully endorsed the view of royal supremacy, not so much from a political standpoint, but because Thomas believed that the monarch was instituted to the throne of England by God[1]. Archbishop Cranmer was a loyal servant of the Crown, in so far as the Crown ruled in accordance with the Word of God. Thomas felt that he was in the right position as the king's spiritual advisor to encourage that to happen. But Thomas was wise enough to know that a true and lasting transformation of the Church of England required prayer, patience and perseverance. It even took time for him to be convinced of the Protestant faith. It was through the diligent and prayerful study of the Scriptures and writings of the early church fathers, and conversations with his reformed continental friends, that over time he too was changed.

You see, Henry had no real intention to deviate from the medieval Catholic Church, not really. He

---

1. See Romans 13:1-7; 1 Timothy 2:1-4.

just wanted the freedom to govern as King of England without papal authority and interference. It was not uncommon for the pope to give out dispensations. He did it all the time. He didn't give one to Henry because he was afraid of Catherine's relatives in Spain. Rome had experienced suppression under the military might of Spain in the past and Clement VII didn't want a repeat of that. And now the English Church was in flux.

It was a man named Cromwell, and not Cranmer, who was the man that the king relied on to put in place his next reform of the church in 1535. The king's gaze was directed towards the wealthy monasteries across his kingdom. An inspection was implemented under the guidance of Cromwell. It was suggested that the monks who lived and worked at the monasteries were corrupt, greedy, and immoral men. Perhaps some of them were. However, the reality had more to do with the wealth and land of the church that could be seized by the Crown and delivered into the king's coffers. And although Archbishop Cranmer was in favour of the inspection, he wanted the seized assets to be used for education and charity in England. He had no delight for the way that the church's estates were distributed to selfish and greedy lords and laymen. He was very disappointed with it all.

The events of the following year proved extremely challenging to the Archbishop of Canterbury. He was to witness the demise of Anne Boleyn. Thomas held Anne in high regard and had much affection for her.

When he was working on the king's cause in the Boleyn home all those years ago, he recalled many insightful and stimulating conversations with her concerning the writings of Martin Luther. She was a good ally in his desire to reform the church.

Not everyone at the king's court felt the same way about her though. At the beginning of the year, she gave birth to a stillborn son. It was such a sad day for the royal family. Thomas did everything he could to console the king and queen in their sorrow. Over the following months, he could see that Henry was becoming more bad-tempered, as he still did not have a son and heir.

Rumours began to circulate in the king's court that Henry was turning his attentions to one of Anne's ladies-in-waiting. Her name was Jane Seymour. Those opposed to a Protestant direction of church and state were quick to seize upon the opportunity to damage a Protestant queen. They made accusations of witchcraft and adultery against her. These were punishable by death. Thomas felt that there was no other option but to speak to the king on her behalf. It was very clear that no one else was going to do it.

The king sat majestically on his throne as he gave permission for the archbishop to be let into his chamber. The king knew that there was no guile in his friend, so he would listen to his counsel.

Thomas approached the king slowly and gracefully. 'Your Majesty, thank you for allowing me to speak with you,' said Thomas respectfully to his monarch.

'What is it, my Lord Archbishop?' asked Henry.

'I am so bewildered that my mind is completely amazed,' he told the king.

'How so?'

'I never had a better opinion of any woman than I had of the queen,' he replied. 'I think that Your Grace knows best that, next unto Your Grace, I was most bound unto her of all living creatures.'

'Go on,' said the king. He could see the anguish on Thomas's face.

'I hope with all my heart that the queen is found without blame and innocent of these charges against her, Your Majesty.'

'My dear Archbishop Cranmer, the queen shall be tried fairly.'

Thomas wanted to believe it, but he was wise to the conspiracies of those in opposition to the queen. They were out for blood, and they would do all they could to have it. His heart was beating just that bit faster as he pushed the king further on the matter. Thomas chose his words very carefully. 'Your Majesty, if I may be so bold to remind you,' he said, 'that your own life is not without blame before our Heavenly Father.'

Although the king knew it to be true, he did not like to be reminded of his shortcomings. He curtly dismissed his archbishop from his presence. Thomas bowed graciously and left.

Anne was taken to the Tower of London by boat on 2nd May 1536. The hearing for her alleged treachery was presided over by her uncle, the Duke of Norfolk. Remarkably, there was no family favouritism shown, as might be expected in such circumstances. It did not take long for the accused and her so-called lovers to be found guilty and sentenced to death. Anne spent the last days of her life in the Tower awaiting her execution. Thomas was greatly saddened that his plea to the king fell on deaf ears. The day of Anne's execution arrived. It was 19th May 1536. She was dressed in black, and good humoured to the end. As she stepped up on to the small wooden platform, she addressed the crowd that had gathered at Tower Green to watch the spectacle.

'The king has been good to me,' she said. 'He promoted me from maid to a marchioness[2]. Then he raised me to be a queen. Now he will raise me to be a martyr[3].' She knelt and prayed, 'To Jesus Christ, I commend my soul; Lord Jesus, receive my soul.' The blow from the sharp sword was swift to the back of her neck. Anne Boleyn was dead.

Thomas looked on, his heart heavy with grief. Anne was the second Queen of England to die that year. Catherine of Aragon passed away on 7th January, 1536. She had fallen ill towards the end of the previous year. The people of England, who held her in high regard, mourned her death. The king, however, did not. The day after Anne's execution, Henry proposed to Jane

---

2. A *marchioness* is a title of nobility.

3. A *martyr* is someone who is killed because of his or her religious beliefs.

Seymour. They were married at a quiet ceremony in the Palace of Whitehall at Westminster on 30th May. Archbishop Cranmer did not officiate at the wedding. Instead, it was Bishop Stephen Gardiner who led the service. That day, Thomas prayed earnestly that this royal marriage would work, for the good of the monarchy and the nation. Come what may, he was the king's loyal servant.

There were more difficult days ahead. Since the start of the year, Archbishop Cranmer had been meeting with his bishops, to bring about a written definition of the Christian faith. It was a hard process. Some people wanted to hang on to the old religion and its ways, and others, like the Archbishop of Canterbury, did not. By June, the process was stuck. So, the king decided to take the matter into his own hands – he was after all, a capable theologian in his own eyes. Henry wrote a series of articles that were a general compromise between the old and the new. His theological champion, Thomas Cranmer, revised the king's work to contain some Lutheran ideas and Convocation gave it the thumbs up in July. The document was called *The Ten Articles*, a first of its kind in the slow journey towards an English Reformation. It was far from perfect, but it did disown the terrible practice of Indulgences. However, it did not change the medieval position on the Lord's Supper, concerning the real presence of Christ's body and blood in the bread and wine. This teaching was called Transubstantiation, and to the continental reformers, it was a most unbiblical position to hold. Although Thomas was by now strongly Protestant, it would take him a few more years to come to their way of understanding the Lord's Supper. He had more study and thinking to do on the matter.

The autumn of 1536 brought yet another problem for Thomas. It concerned the closure of monasteries across England. By November, forty thousand men went on the march in Yorkshire, protesting the seizure of church land and money by the Crown. The revolt was known as a 'pilgrimage of grace' because they wanted the king to know that they were not rebelling against him. They did, however, have a list of demands. The agitators wanted the reunion of the English Church to Rome and the restoration of Princess Mary as the rightful heir of the throne. They viewed the Archbishop of Canterbury as the patron of heretics[4] and the author of Catherine's divorce from Henry. They wanted him locked up in the Tower, or failing that, booted out of England. A bonus would be the dismissal of the chief instigator of the closures, Thomas Cromwell.

Well, the king would have none of it! He quelled the rebellion by sending some of his own army north. The noble leaders of the rebellion were arrested and executed, effectively destroying any further opposition to Thomas Cranmer and his reforms for the remainder of the king's reign. This was the turning point in the

---

4. A *heretic* is someone who holds a belief that is in opposition to the established Church of Rome.

religious life of England. And what is more, Thomas Cromwell had issued a set of commands in connection with *The Ten Articles*. By the end of the year, they were beginning to bear fruit, especially the one that required every parish priest to get a copy of the Bible in English and Latin before the end of the summer months of 1537.

Thomas could not contain his delight when a copy of the Scriptures in English was placed into his hands. He sat down at his desk in Lambeth Palace to pen a letter to Cromwell. He said that the Bible was more to his liking than any other translation made so far. He begged Cromwell to get the king's permission for its sale and for it to be read by everyone in England. It did not take Cromwell long to get the king's consent. When Thomas found out, he wrote him another letter:

'My Lord, thank you for going to all the trouble to make this happen. Be assured, your Lordship, that even if you had given me a thousand pounds, I would still not be as happy as I am about the Bible. I do not doubt that your actions shall bear good fruit in England. You have done such high and acceptable service unto God and the king.'

Cranmer could now see that the mists of ignorance and idolatry were slowly starting to lift in his English Reformation.

Cranmer's Bible

Once again, the plague was taking its toll on England. It broke out in the summer of 1537 and by the autumn, many had taken flight to safer havens in the countryside.

Cranmer met Cromwell at his Putney residence. 'They die almost everywhere in London,' Thomas told his friend, 'and in Lambeth, they die at my gate.'

'Perhaps it is time to move to somewhere safer,' suggested Cromwell. 'Already the plague has driven the king to Esher.' The palace there was only three miles from Hampton Court. Far enough from the plague but close enough for any emergency in London. Thomas thought it was a bold move, considering the queen was still in Hampton Court and due to have a baby any day.

'His Majesty has given orders to his physicians to look after the queen. I have been instructed to call for him when the baby arrives,' said Cromwell.

'I hope that Her Majesty does not have too arduous a labour,' said Thomas. 'I pray constantly that mother and child will be well through it all.'

On 12th October Queen Jane gave birth to a healthy boy. When the king heard the news, he rode jubilantly to Hampton Court. His entourage could hardly keep up with him. He ordered celebrations throughout the land. He had his son and heir. There was no greater reason to make merry than that.

They decided to call him Edward. But the boy's mother became sick after bringing him into the world. Cranmer constantly visited her bedside to pray for her and bring her what comfort he could from the Word of God. But Jane only had twelve days with her baby boy, before she passed away. Although she had been Queen of England for a short time, the nation liked her, and mourned her. As for Henry, he was devastated. In his grief he retreated to the palace of Esher in Surrey. There was little anyone could say to ease his pain. But Thomas, his trusted archbishop, knew that his own words would bring little consolation. Only the words of hope from the One who had conquered death, the Lord Jesus Christ, would be fitting in this dire circumstance.

In the luxurious drawing room of his stately home, the king sat staring into the flames of the roaring fire. The logs spat and hissed as the flames engulfed them. Thomas sat opposite Henry and watched his friend's still form in the firelight.

'Your Majesty,' he said softly. 'My words can offer you little comfort. There is One greater than I whose words, however, bring hope in the midst of pain.'

Henry turned his head for a moment to look at the anguished face of his trusted archbishop. But he did not hold his gaze. He looked again into the flames dancing in the grate before him.

Thomas opened his Bible and began to read Psalm 23 thoughtfully. The words were like soothing ointment on a gaping wound. 'Even though I walk through the valley of the shadow of death, I will fear no evil, for you are with me; your rod and your staff, they comfort me[1].' Thomas paused. 'Your Majesty,' he said gently, 'in all my years reading and studying the Bible, I know that it never says that God will spare us from trouble and grief. You know this to be true in your own life,' he said, then slowly added, 'as do I.'

The king was motionless, but Thomas knew he was listening. He chose his words carefully. 'In the words of this Psalm, Your Majesty, we have the Almighty's promise of his own company with us in this hard world. And he promises hope for an everlasting future, that will triumph even over the grave, for those who trust in him.'

Thomas waited to see if the king wanted to say something …anything. But Henry was contented to allow his pastor to counsel him in his time of sorrow. Thomas knew his monarch's silence was permission to continue.

'Our Lord Jesus Christ called himself the Good Shepherd, who laid down his life for the sheep[2]. As we

---

1. Psalm 23:4 ESV.
2. John 10:14-15.

trust in him, Your Majesty, knowing what he has done for us on that cruel cross, we can know him personally and be known by him. His presence is with us always, to guide and govern us in this world and the next. And this is the comfort that the Lord wants us to know in our grief ... and especially in your grief, Your Majesty.'

Henry turned his head and looked directly into the eyes of his archbishop. His demeanour was quiet. 'Thank you for your words of comfort, Thomas,' he said. 'My heart is full of sadness, indeed.' The king moved forward in his seat and sighed. 'I am also relieved, Thomas,' he whispered.

'Relieved, Your Majesty?' said Thomas with mild curiosity. He had been with the king long enough to guess what he was about to say.

'That I have a son, who is healthy, at last,' replied Henry.

'He will make a fine king,' said Thomas and smiled warmly.

'Yes, he will,' breathed Henry, as he settled back into his chair again to watch the dancing flames in the fireplace. Sometimes it is difficult to move on with life after bereavement, but by the grace of God, Henry did.

In 1539 a new revised version of the Bible was brought out in Paris. It was nicknamed 'The Great Bible' because it was so big. The Archbishop of Canterbury expected every church in England to have a copy of it within twelve months of its publication.

He wanted to secure the widest reading of this book as the Word of God. It was printed again in 1540 and 1541, and by then, Thomas had written the book's introduction. In it, he encouraged 'all who come to hear or read this Book, which is the Word of God, the most precious jewel and most holy relic that remains upon earth, that you bring with you the fear of God, and that you do it with all due reverence, and use your knowledge of the Word of God, not for the sake of your pride in winning silly arguments, but for the honour of God, the increase of goodness and the improvement of yourself and others.' 'The Great Bible' became known as Cranmer's Bible.

This new measure in the Church of England was another step along the slow path to reform. But sometimes it seems like one step forward can be followed by two steps back. The same year of the release of 'The Great Bible', the king wanted to devise another uniform standard of faith, like the one that came into existence a few years ago. A small group of Lords were assembled to work on the new document, but they couldn't agree. Henry decided to help them, after all, he was a theologian too, or so he thought. In the House of Lords, he dazzled, or, perhaps more accurately he confused the committee with his learning. Thomas would have none of it! At every point of disagreement, he stood to dispute his monarch. It felt like Thomas never sat down, as the king was still holding on to the old ways. Henry wanted to keep the Mass and the belief that the bread and wine turned into Christ's real flesh and blood during the sacrament. He wanted to affirm that a priest should never marry. And that anyone who preaches or teaches anything contrary to his statements of doctrine should be tried and burned for heresy!

The spectators were amazed at Thomas's intellect and courage and stupidity. Did he not see the king was getting irked by his persistent challenging? Inwardly some egged Thomas on in the hope that he would get himself into trouble with an increasingly bad-tempered monarch. They didn't like the changes Archbishop Cranmer was making in the Church. Exasperated by his archbishop's opposition, Henry ordered Thomas to leave the meeting! It was only when Thomas was out of the room that the king had his way, and the new document called the *Six Articles* was passed into law. Those who leaned towards a Protestant understanding of the Christian faith saw it as a defeat. Some who were bishops, resigned their positions. Thomas Cranmer was convinced in his own mind that the document would never have passed, had the king not come down to the House of Lords in person. It was possible that he had underestimated the strength of opposition to his reforms that still existed.

For his part, Henry never asked Thomas to change his personal views, nor did he remove him from his archbishopric. He had a genuine respect for Cranmer's great knowledge of the Bible and the writings of the early church fathers. There was a real and genuine bond between him and Thomas. Henry knew that Thomas's loyalty was not just to the Crown, but to him personally. He was grateful to Thomas for his help with his Great Cause. And he liked Thomas. He was so different to everyone else in court. It was abundantly clear to the king that Thomas was sincere. He had no personal ambitions, no desire for wealth, and he wasn't devious like some others he knew. There was no deceit in Thomas, and he was always ready to forgive. He had the ability of understanding the point of view of any opponent which made him sympathetic to their plight, even if he didn't agree with them. Thomas could say anything to the king, and it would not end in his demise. Cromwell told Cranmer the same thing.

'You were born in a happy hour; for do and say what you will, the king will always take it well at your hand. And I must confess that in some things I have complained of you to His Majesty, but all in vain, for he will never give credit against you, whatever is laid to your charge; but let me or any other of the council be complained of, His Grace will most seriously chide and fall out with us. And therefore, you are most happy if you can keep you in this estate.'

Cromwell was very perceptive. He proved his own words true when the king struck against him with the ruthless ease of a bird of prey. Cromwell had encouraged the king to marry once again and to look overseas for a new bride. At the beginning of 1540, the king was wed to Anne of Cleves. She was the sister of a German prince called Wilhelm Duke of Cleves. Although he was not a member of the evangelical Schmalkaldic league[3], his friends were. Neither he, nor they, liked the papacy or the Holy Roman Empire. Cromwell saw it as an opportunity for England to renew its acquaintance with the continental reformers and perhaps get the reform of the Church of England moving forward again.

Sadly, the king's marriage failed. In June, Cromwell was arrested for treason and housed in the Tower of London. All his friends and allies quickly faded away, all except Thomas. He wrote to the king at once. He told Henry that Thomas Cromwell 'was such a servant, in my judgement, in wisdom, diligence, faithfulness, and experience, as no prince in this realm ever had. I loved him as my friend, that is what I took him to be; but I chiefly loved him for the love which I thought I saw him bear ever towards Your Grace, singularly above all other.' It was very brave of Thomas to write such a thing, as he was a lone voice on behalf of Thomas Cromwell, the Earl of Essex, the 'traitor'. However, it did not matter. Cromwell was executed on the morning of 28th July at Tower Hill. The axe was blunt, and he died in great pain.

In the cause of Reformation, Thomas Cranmer now had to stand alone.

---

3. *The Schmalkaldic League* began in Schmalkden, Germany. It was a group of rulers within the Holy Roman Empire who were not happy with the Catholic Church and embraced the reformed teaching advocated by the German Reformer, Martin Luther.

A True Friend

Danger was all around Thomas. It was the perfect time to strike the lone reformer. Cranmer felt like the prophet Elijah who was pitted against the prophets of Baal in 1 Kings[1]. Elijah thought he was the only servant of the Lord left, but he wasn't. God had many others; it was just that Elijah didn't know about them.

For Thomas, there was support for his reforms, and even though Thomas felt alone, he wasn't. He knew that God was with him and he trusted that God had a plan for the Church in England.

Cranmer's contemporary and former colleague in the king's great cause, Bishop Stephen Gardiner, stepped up to secretly lead the assault on the Archbishop of Canterbury. His aim was to disgrace Thomas in the eyes of the king, and if he accomplished the death penalty for heresy or treason, even better! And the more isolated Cranmer felt, the easier it would be to bring about his downfall.

---

1. 1 Kings 18:22; 19:10, 14, 18.

In April 1542 the Chapter of Canterbury Cathedral[2] in Kent, received the king's permission to allow for twelve new Prebendaries[3] to join its numbers. Out of the new members only one was an ally of reform. His name was Nicholas Ridley. The remainder did not care much for what Cranmer was doing to their beloved Catholic Church in England. They wanted to remain with Rome. Gardiner soon found some Kentish noblemen who were also deeply annoyed with the changes in the Church's teaching and practice that the Archbishop of Canterbury had been introducing. The plot against Thomas thickened as two clergy from Kent rode to London the following spring, with a list of accusations against him.

The antagonists underestimated the king's insight regarding the minds of his servants. And Henry would certainly not be used by anyone to advance their own cause. He decided to keep his thoughts to himself until he had the chance to row down the River Thames past Lambeth Palace. It was not uncommon when the king left Hampton Court to use the Thames to get up to London. His royal barge was large, ornate and sheltered at one end for the comfort of the monarch. It was powered by an even number of rowers who maintained a steady but gentle pace on the water. The

---

2. The **Chapter of Canterbury Cathedral** was a body of clergy who advised and assisted the Archbishop of Canterbury at the Cathedral church.

3. A **Prebendary** is a member of the clergy who helps administrate the workings of a Cathedral church.

king loved music and usually on his barge trips he was accompanied by musicians who played sweetly so as not to offend the royal ears.

Cranmer was at home in Lambeth the day the king was passing by. He heard the music from the royal barge and walked down the pathway to the steps at the side of the river. He wanted to pay his respects to His Majesty.

Henry ordered the barge to stop at the place where his archbishop was standing. As it came to a halt, Thomas bowed his head and greeted his king enthusiastically.

'Your Majesty, you have picked a splendid day for a boat trip.'

'Yes, indeed, Archbishop!' exclaimed the king. 'The sun is shining and the elements are calm. Step aboard and accompany me for a short while.'

Thomas was helped on to the barge by a servant and led to a chair opposite the king. Thomas could see from the way that the king was looking at him as he sat down, that His Majesty had something to tell him.

'I have news for you, my Lord' began Henry. 'I now know who the greatest heretic is in Kent.'

The archbishop's eyes widened. 'Who is it, Your Grace?' he asked, inquisitively.

The king pulled a parchment from his sleeve. 'I have his name and a list of charges against him on this paper.' Henry slowly opened the folded sheets of paper and squinted at the writing on it. He was, of course, doing it for dramatic effect. He could see plainly what was written, but he was enjoying the suspense of the moment, and the look of curiosity on Thomas's face.

'This devilish man works in Canterbury,' Henry said, mischievously.

I work in Canterbury. I wonder if I know him, thought Thomas. He began to think of all his clergy in the Cathedral. As far as he was concerned, there were certainly a few who fit the description. Superstitious men of limited theological intellect, doing the work of the Father of lies[4] and leading men, women, boys, and girls astray from the narrow path that leads to life in Christ alone[5].

Then Thomas took a sharp intake of breath. Does the king mean me? He knew that his own prebendaries at the Cathedral Church in Canterbury had no love for him. Now that Cromwell was gone, they were more open in their opposition to his reforms. In their opinion, the Archbishop of Canterbury was wrecking the Catholic Church.

'The penny has dropped, has it Thomas?' asked the king.

'So, I am the greatest heretic in Kent, Your Grace,' said Thomas, seeking the king's confirmation to his statement.

'Apparently so. Let me enlighten you of the charges placed against you.' Henry began to read a list of complaints against Thomas and his few allies at

---

4. John 8:44.
5. Matthew 7:13-14.

Canterbury Cathedral, like Nicholas Ridley. Although the king was enjoying the humour of the moment at his friend's expense, he would not be swayed by the complaints made against his archbishop. He knew fine well that Thomas was a good and loyal man.

The real interest of the document lay with the signatories. Henry read those out too. The charges were made by some noblemen from Kent and the prebendaries of his own Cathedral in Canterbury. When the king had finished reading, Thomas spoke up.

'Your Majesty, the charges made by these men vex me. May I request that Your Majesty set up a Commission of Inquiry to investigate the truth or not of these concerns?'

'Splendid idea, Archbishop. And I propose that you head up the Inquiry into these matters.'

'Your Grace, as I am the person accused of these things, surely it would be fitting and proper to have someone else do it?'

'My Lord Archbishop. I do not trust anyone enough to investigate these charges fairly. And I know that you will, even if they are against you. Appoint the people you see fit for the Commission. And you can report your findings when the investigation is over.' Henry's trust in Thomas was steadfast.

The barge returned to Lambeth Palace and Thomas disembarked. He went to work setting up the Commission of Inquiry immediately. He even invited some of his accusers from the Cathedral to be part of it.

Days turned into weeks, and there was no progress to report to the king. Soon after, the plot was exposed for the farce it was. What was the king going to do with the instigators of such a devious plot to bring down his archbishop? It was decided to let Archbishop Cranmer divvy out a suitable punishment for their crimes. Most of them came before Thomas expressing their deep sorrow and regret for their callous treatment of him. They wanted him dead, or at the very least, disgraced and ousted from his position as Archbishop of Canterbury. But now they were full of sorrow and pleading for their lives. Thomas knew what the king would do with such treachery in his courtiers. But he was not Henry. He wanted to be like his Lord and Saviour Jesus Christ. So, Thomas forgave his accusers and sent them away with words of kindness and comfort. The king was not surprised with such leniency from his archbishop. It was in keeping with his good nature.

The next attempt to discredit Archbishop Cranmer and bring him to ruin was the most serious of all. Some members of the king's Privy Council[6] asked to have Cranmer committed to the Tower of London. They reasoned that no one would dare accuse a man of such high standing in the king's court if he were not imprisoned. Astonishingly the king agreed that they should carry out the deed the following day. However,

---

6. *The Privy Council* formally advised the king on matters of interest to the Royal Family.

that night, at eleven o'clock, the king summoned Cranmer.

'My Lord Archbishop, I have news that will unsettle you,' began the king. 'There is another plot against you.'

'Another one, Your Majesty?'

'I will speak plainly to you. Some of my Privy Council have requested that you be imprisoned in the Tower. They argue that no one will dare accuse you of heresy and treason while you enjoy freedom.'

'May I express my most hearty thanks to Your Majesty for telling me of this plot against me. If it please Your Majesty, I will happily go to the Tower, if it aids a fair hearing.'

'What fond simplicity have you, to permit yourself to be imprisoned that every enemy of yours may take advantage against you!' cried Henry.

Thomas looked rather sheepishly at his king, who continued, 'do you not know that when they have you once in prison, three or four false knaves will soon be procured to witness against you and condemn you; which, now being at liberty, dare not once open their lips or appear before your face? No, not so my lord: I have better regard for you than to permit your enemies so to overthrow you.'

'Forgive me, Your Majesty,' replied Thomas. 'What is your counsel?'

'Tomorrow morning, they will order you to the Privy Council Chamber. When they have you before them, ask to be brought face to face with your accusers.

If they refuse your request and proceed to commit you to the Tower, make an appeal direct to the Throne.'

Henry took a ring off his finger and handed it to Thomas. 'Give them this ring,' he said. 'They know it well enough. It is the ring that I use for no other purpose than to call matters from the Privy Council into my own hands.'

Thomas was moved by Henry's kindness to him. 'Your Majesty, I am lost for words. Thank you for your wisdom and your protection.'

At eight o'clock the next morning, Thomas received his summons to come before the Privy Council. On his arrival, he was instructed to stand outside the door in the company of the servants. The king found out about this and was angered by the news. 'Have they served my lord so?' he exclaimed to the messenger. 'I will have a word with them shortly.'

After waiting outside the Privy Council door for half an hour, Cranmer was called inside the chamber.

'My Lord Archbishop,' began the chief councillor. 'It is the king's will that you should be taken to the Tower at once and held there until your trial for heresy commences.'

'I humbly request that I be allowed to address my accusers face to face,' said Thomas. 'It is only fair. Do you not agree?'

'That is completely out of the question, Archbishop!' exclaimed the councillor. 'Surely you understand that a man of your high office would only intimidate your accusers into silence. No. I am afraid your request will not be granted.'

'That is regrettable,' said Thomas. He paused for a moment then he said in a strong voice, 'I am sorry my lords that you drive me to this urgently. I must now appeal from you to the King's Majesty, who by this token of a ring, has returned this matter into his own hand, and discharged you of this duty immediately.'

Thomas pulled the king's special ring out of his sleeve and held it up high for the council to see. In frustration, one of the councillors cried out: 'We might have known that the king would not allow him to go to prison!'

The chamber was in uproar, causing some of the council members to go hastily to the king and demand he retract his protection of Cranmer. The king scolded them for their conspiracies against the archbishop. Then in a calm voice, he said, 'you should well understand that I believe my lord of Canterbury is as faithful a man towards me as there ever was a bishop in this realm. And because of him, I am, in many ways, grateful for the faith I have in God; and therefore, whoever loves me will look upon him in the same way.'

This was the last time anyone plotted against Thomas Cranmer during the remainder of Henry's reign.

King is Dead

The King is Dead,
Long Live the King!

The ailing king lay in his bed. His speech was weak as he whispered to his closest courtier to send for the Archbishop of Canterbury. When the news was relayed to Thomas that Henry was close to the end, he made haste to the king's bedside. It was the early hours of the morning of 28th January 1547, when Thomas arrived at the king's bedchamber in the inner sanctum of Whitehall Palace in London. Henry no longer had the strength to speak. Upon seeing Thomas enter the room, Henry reached out his hand. Thomas grasped it and slowly knelt at the king's bedside.

For all his dictatorial and ruthless ways, Henry and Thomas really were true friends. Many in the king's court rose to dominance and then fell from such lofty heights, some with a drastic end like Thomas Cromwell. But there was one man towards whom the king's heart never seemed to waver; that man was Thomas Cranmer. Henry knew that he could search his realm in vain for a man like Cranmer. His archbishop was unlike other men who held such a high office in the Church. Henry loved his honesty and his extensive learning. There was no trace of self-seeking ambition in Thomas, as there was in statesmen like Wolsey. Henry admired the fact that Thomas did not lust after wealth or power, and that he was not afraid to beg him for mercy on behalf of a friend or enemy with little regard for his own safety. Indeed, there can be no doubt that a deep friendship grew between the two men.

'I came as quickly as I could, Your Majesty,' he gently said. The king nodded his head faintly. 'You are not long for this world, Henry. I urge you to put your trust in Christ and ask him to be merciful unto you.' Thomas looked at the face of his dying friend. 'Give me some token with your eyes or with this grasped hand that you trust in the Lord.' Thomas could feel the king's grip of his hand tighten.

Thomas began to pray for the king: 'O God, our refuge and strength, a very present help in times of trouble; be near to this your servant in the greatness of his need. Increase in him a sure faith in your power and a joyful trust in your love. If it is your will to call him heavenward, lessen all pain of body and anguish of mind and grant that he may enter the joy of your eternal presence, through the merits and mediation of Jesus Christ our Lord. Amen.'

Moments later, the king was dead. His children wept for hours when they learned of their father's passing that day. Even the good archbishop was genuinely grieved by the death of the king, although he knew many a crocodile tear[1] would be shed at the king's court. As a mark of sorrow at the king's passing, Thomas decided that he would grow a beard until his own death, no matter how near or far away it was. It was also a statement against the clean-shaven priesthood of the Catholic Church.

Less than a month after King Henry VIII's demise, the coronation of the young Edward VI took place at Westminster Abbey in London on February 20th, 1547. The new king was only nine years old. It was a magnificent and earnest occasion. The Abbey was adorned with tapestries on the walls and the aisles were laid with rushes. Trumpets sounded as Cranmer crowned the new monarch with the traditional three crowns: first, the crown of St Edward, then the state crown which the young king would wear on state occasions, and lastly a 'rich crown' that was made especially for the child king. Thomas then placed a gold ring on Edward's wedding-ring finger of the left hand as a symbol of his kingly majesty.

Thomas knew that Edward had been brought up mainly by nurses, but his stepmother who was also Henry's sixth wife, Catherine Parr, made sure that Edward had the best tutors in the land. The young boy who sat solemnly on the throne before Archbishop Cranmer was good at languages, such as Greek, Latin and French. Edward had made a deep study of the reformation, which was sweeping northern Europe. And he embraced its teachings. At last, a true ally to

---

1. 'Crocodile tears' are cried by those who are insincere in their sorrow.

reform sat on the throne in England. Thomas Cranmer was hopeful that his plans to completely transform the Church of England would soon come to pass under the reign of Edward VI.

The Archbishop of Canterbury climbed into the pulpit of the Abbey and spoke powerfully, imploring all present to put their trust in God and worship him alone. He berated the medieval catholic practice of worshipping saintly images[2] and declared war on the false doctrines espoused by Rome. The young king approved of his archbishop. He felt confident that they would get along wonderfully.

As Edward was so young, his father had made provision in his will for a special group of people to gather around Edward, to advise him and help run the country. It was right and fitting that the Archbishop of Canterbury should be part of this new council. His uncle, Edward Seymour, was made the Duke of Somerset. He was then appointed to the role of Protector of the kingdom, until the king was old enough to effectively rule himself. Thomas Cranmer trusted the Duke of Somerset, because he held Protestant sympathies and would be open to reforming the Church in England. And under the new king, Cranmer set to work to bring about the changes that were so desperately needed in the religious life of the country.

It was common knowledge that the standard of preaching in the Church was quite poor. So, Thomas

---

2. See Fact File at the back of the book.

wrote a *Book of Homilies*[3], to help the clergy preach the Bible faithfully and obediently. It was vital for the spiritual health of each person, and indeed the nation.

At the end of the year, Edward held his first meeting of parliament. The document called the *Six Articles* that was penned by King Henry in 1539 and passed by Convocation and parliament, was overturned. People would no longer be burned at the stake for heresy. And clergy could now legally marry. Result! Mrs Cranmer could at long last come in from the cold! The door of reform was beginning to swing open, much to Cranmer's delight.

Thomas felt that he now needed to encourage some of the reformers in Europe to move to England and take up teaching positions in churches and universities in the country. He had been writing to some of them for years, like Andreas Osiander, and Martin Luther's friend, Philip Melanchthon. He wanted to develop a deep fellowship between them and hoped that they would help him in his efforts to reform the Church in England. They certainly saw Cranmer as the key ally of reform in England. In 1548 a small group of them came and found comfortable lodgings in Cranmer's massive home in Lambeth, until each one was settled into life in England.

These men saw Cranmer's daily routine and they were impressed all the more by his dedication to the study of the Bible and prayer. It was noted that on occasion,

---

3. The **Book of Homilies** was a book of sermons that taught the Bible clearly and faithfully. The clergy would pick a sermon from the book and preach it on Sunday mornings during the church service.

Thomas would get out of bed at two or three in the morning to study the Word of God and to read some of the writings of the early church fathers. But it was more usual for Thomas to be up at five and spend four hours praying and studying. His learning was vast. When King Henry was alive, he loved the fact that if he needed an answer on any theological matter, he could get it the next day if he asked his trusted archbishop. Any other chaplain to the king would require much longer to deliberate and advise His Majesty.

After nine in the morning, Thomas would give his attention to any matters of Church and State. He would welcome friends and callers until lunch. There was always time for a game of chess after that. Then he would hit the books again, preferring to stand at his desk rather than sit. Around five in the afternoon he would go to the private chapel in his home and read the service of Common Prayer. After that, he would take a walk in the gardens until supper time. Another walk and a bit more study before bed around nine p.m. Clearly, Thomas was a resilient man of routine.

His years of study and debate, and his conversations with men such as Nicholas Ridley, led Cranmer to finally abandon the controversial doctrine of transubstantiation; the belief that the bread and wine at the Lord's Supper changes into the real presence of the body and blood of Christ. Thomas came to the conclusion that this teaching was unbiblical and untrue. But many of his church leaders still held on to the old ways of the medieval Church, and especially the doctrine of transubstantiation at the Mass. To change the teachings of the Mass would be a step too far for them. Thomas needed to devise a church Communion service that would bring in the new, while not shutting the door on the old. The new order of Communion was therefore a compromise between the old ways and the new, and it highlighted the need for Cranmer to revise the existing services that were in use. He had been working privately on a single Book of Common Prayer for some time, and it was his desire to see it used in churches throughout the land.

By the end of 1548, Thomas presented a first draft of his book to a group of bishops who had gathered at Windsor, twenty-five miles west of Lambeth Palace. He wanted them to approve his work. He did not want them to suggest changes to it. Most of them thought it was ok. The real test of approval would come from the House of Commons and the House of Lords in London. The book that Thomas presented was a compromise even in his own eyes, but it was a start in the right direction. Opposition to it was more vocal in the Commons. The people who feared change and opposed it, fought tooth and nail to block it. But in the House of Lords, Cranmer and Ridley argued so persuasively and graciously that they won many of the Lords over to the changes that the archbishop had presented before them in his new *Book of Common Prayer*.

As expected, much of the debate focused on the Lord's Supper and the real presence of Christ in the bread and wine. This was not a trivial thing for the medieval church. It was more than just a slight difference of opinion. It struck at the very heart of Roman Catholicism and its theology of the sacrament.

Thomas was shrewd enough to realise that the first draft of his new book was always going to be revised over time. And when Stephen Gardiner, the Bishop of Winchester, said that he would gladly use the new form of service for Communion, Thomas realised that his changes had not gone far enough! More were needed, sooner rather than later!

'My Lord Archbishop. Are you not pleased with the outcome today?' asked Nicholas Ridley as they walked from the great entrance doors of the House of Lords.

'I thought that you spoke very well, Nicholas,' replied the archbishop, 'but I fear that we are far from done in our quest to reform the church. There are many to convince. They still hold on to the old ways.'

'The king is an ally of reform,' said Nicholas. 'Surely that is in our favour?'

'Yes, indeed, and we must make hay while the sun shines, Nicholas,' retorted Thomas.

The New Prayer Book

The parliament of young King Edward passed a law[1] that enforced the use of Cranmer's *Book of Common Prayer* in January 1549. Anyone who refused to use the new book, or said anything derogatory about it or its contents, faced fines or imprisonment. Three offences and they were out of ministry and in prison, for life!

The *Book of Common Prayer* was not an instant hit, even with the leaders of the Reformation. It was trying to do a difficult job of bringing two opposing parties, the adherents to Catholicism and the Reformers, together under one roof, or at least travelling in the same direction. Thomas did not want to alienate the conservatives of the old ways. He really did want to bring them with him in his mission of change. But it was a dangerous journey, fraught with many obstacles, like pride. The first *Book of Common Prayer* was always going to be a compromise in need of further work, and it would get an overhaul in due time. But it was a good

1. The law was called the *Act of Uniformity*. This Act established the 1549 Book of Common Prayer as the only lawful form of corporate worship in the Church of England.

place to begin the journey together. The weakness of the book was seen in the service of Communion. Both parties could interpret it according to their different positions. The only course of action for Cranmer was to set about revising the book so that it expressed the true scriptural position of the Lord's Supper.

The church services were often noisy and chaotic. The priest stood at the chancel, which was the name given to the east end of the church building. The altar was also situated in the chancel, and it was the focus of the service. The altar had a crucifix on it which was a representation of Jesus on the cross. The chancel was separate from the nave. The nave was the main body of the church building where the congregation stood or sat. There were no pews or chairs for ordinary people. Only the wealthy and infirm got a chair to sit on. There were, of course, seats for the priests in the chancel area. The congregation just milled about chatting to each other, as they didn't understand what the priest was saying. Most of them couldn't read either. That is why the walls were covered in brightly coloured paintings of religious scenes to help the people understand something of the Christian message. The main thrust was good works get you to heaven, and bad works cast you down to hell where terrible things happened to you.

The nave and the chancel were separated by a screen called a rood screen. The congregation in the nave could hardly see into the chancel, which was the holiest part of the church. They could not see the priest's special connection with God during the service. The rood screen was made of wood or stone. From the altar, the priest would recite the Mass in Latin. Ordinary English folk did not understand the language. But it was generally felt that the Latin words carried a form of mystical power. The vague outline of the priest could be seen through the rood, as he held up the bread and, in a voice barely audible, he said, '*hoc est corpus meum*,' meaning 'this is my body.' These were the words Jesus Christ spoke when he broke the bread at the Last Supper. Those who could not see what was happening, nor hear what was being said, would sometimes ask another in the congregation what the priest was doing. The reply often came, 'he is doing his *hocus pocus* bit.' It was the magical transformation of the bread into the real body of Jesus, or so they were led to believe.

Thomas Cranmer wanted to teach the truth of the Scriptures in a simple way that everyone could understand. The soul of the nation was at stake. Therefore, the new book was written in English rather than Latin, so that people could understand what was being said. He also steeped the new *Prayer Book* in Scripture. His desire was that the citizens of the realm would hear, read (if they knew how to) and inwardly digest the Word of God. He wanted them to come to a true knowledge of God and of his Son, Jesus Christ, the Lord and Saviour of the world. It was why the pulpit became so important in the fabric of church buildings across the land. Thomas wanted the pulpit placed at the front of the nave so that the priest could preach directly to the people in English, and not through a rood screen. With the emphasis now on preaching it became necessary to provide seating for everyone. Pews were gradually introduced into the naves and aisles of church buildings.

Archbishop Cranmer prayed earnestly that the Holy Spirit of God would take the preached Word of God and open the blind eyes of men, women, boys, and girls throughout the country, so that they could see Jesus and know him personally. Thomas prayed that he would be a good servant of Christ and His mission to the lost souls of King Edward's dominion.

The Lord provided him help in his task. The Duke of Somerset, Edward Seymour, was also a reformer. Cranmer enjoyed working with him. But Cranmer's former colleague in the king's Great Cause, Stephen Gardiner, the Bishop of Winchester, was now very vocal in his disapproval of the archbishop's changes. He had written over twenty letters of complaint to Somerset, arguing that the reforms being introduced were scripturally wrong and unlawful. His constant opposition resulted in his incarceration at the Tower of London. However, nothing would deter him from objecting to the English Reformation.

'I will not be silenced,' declared Gardiner to the jailer.

'Keep this up and it will not just be your tongue that you lose, Bishop,' said the jailer. 'Here, this was brought for you. A bit of light reading.' The jailer tossed a document to Gardiner who picked it up and read the title. 'A Defence of the True and Catholic Doctrine of the Sacrament, by the Most Reverend Thomas Cranmer, by Divine Providence Lord Archbishop of Canterbury.' Gardiner started to leaf through the pages quickly.

'I want some parchment and a quill!' demanded Gardiner, 'and ink! The *good* archbishop has written this document.' He held it up and through gritted teeth, he angrily read, '"A Defence of the True and Catholic Doctrine of the Sacrament." I'll give him a defence alright,' he said. 'Bring me some parchment!'

'Of course,' said the jailer, smiling as he walked away from the cell. He enjoyed moments like this.

'And a quill!' shouted Gardiner after him. But the jailer was gone. Gardiner started to mutter under his breath. 'You wait and see, Thomas Cranmer. I will have my say. And one day, you will sit where I now sit.'

Gardiner took his time to reply to Cranmer's arguments for a true biblical defence of the Lord's Supper. He decided to call his work, *A Confutation*. He aimed to prove that Cranmer was wrong in his thinking about the Lord's Supper. It was published later the same year as Cranmer's Defence, in 1550. His tactic was to imply that Cranmer didn't write the *Defence* in the first place because it expressed views that were so hostile to the position that he was known to have had all those years ago – the same views that Gardiner held so dearly. Gardiner then ably explained the Roman Catholic teaching of the Mass and the Communion.

The following year, Cranmer penned a reply to his adversary's *Confutation* and called it, *An Answer*. In his *Answer*, Thomas said, 'I am glad, even from the bottom of my heart that it has pleased Almighty God in this latter end of my years to give me knowledge of my former error and a will to embrace the truth.' He stressed that the presence of Christ at the Lord's Supper was a spiritual reality, known by faith alone in the heart of the person.

The need for the reform of church services was made evident by the disputes which followed the *Prayer Book* of 1549. However, it could not be denied that the people of England had been given a great gift of common prayer, as opposed to the many and varied church service books available before its publication. Not only that, but it was also written in the language of the people instead of Latin. For the first time men and women throughout the realm of England could join in corporate worship at the parish church with understanding and unity. This was a great blessing to England. Yet there were still uncertainties about doctrine. Some of the language was open to interpretation, which suited those who loved the old traditional unreformed ways. So, with the help of some reformed friends like Nicholas Ridley, who was now the Bishop of London, Thomas Cranmer began to work on a second *Book of Common Prayer*.

The month of January in 1552 heralded a new dawn in the life of the Church of England. A second law of King Edward's parliament[2] was passed for the use of a new *Book of Common Prayer*. The difference between this book and the former 1549 *Book of Common Prayer* was that it removed any doubt about its reformed doctrinal position. The service of the Lord's Supper was so clearly Protestant, there could be no grounds for open interpretation from those like Stephen Gardiner, who held on to the old traditional religion of England. Cranmer's mastery of the English language made the new *Prayer Book* excel in dignity and devotion, unlike anything that had been written before or even since. The very substance of the 1552 *Prayer Book* lives on in Anglican worship around the world today.

The passing of this second law also declared it a crime when people '*wilfully and damnably before Almighty God abstain and refuse to come to their parish churches*'! The punishment for skipping church without a very good excuse was left to church officials. It was illegal to use any form of church service other than the 1552 *Book of Common Prayer*. If someone was caught doing so, for a first offence, the penalty was imprisonment for six months without bail. For a second offence, it was imprisonment for a year without bail and for a third, life imprisonment!

---

2. The second *Act of Uniformity* was approved in 1552. It made the new *Book of Common Prayer* the only lawful book for corporate worship in the Church of England

The beheading of Edward Seymour, the Duke of Somerset, on the 22nd of January 1552 was also extremely harsh. The young King Edward wrote in his diary: '*The Duke of Somerset had his head cut off on Tower Hill between 8 and 9 o'clock in the morning.*' Somerset was the victim of false evidence which solidified his conviction on trumped-up charges of treason and law-breaking. King Edward's attention had been diverted away from his uncle's plight. John Dudley, the Duke of Northumberland, used Christmas festivities to keep the boy king occupied. The death of the Duke of Somerset eliminated the serious threat of opposition he posed to the new protector, Northumberland.

Thomas was saddened deeply by the execution of Edward Seymour. Under the Duke's leadership, he had witnessed the relaxation of heresy laws which meant that clergy could have proper discussions on those issues which divided them, without fear of imprisonment or execution if they disagreed with the government. Clergy had also been released from the burden of compulsory celibacy. The Mass had been replaced by an English service of the Lord's Supper. And the Church of England had been given a service book that edified and encouraged the people in their corporate worship of Almighty God. And let's not forget the introduction of a Bible in English into every parish church in England during the leadership of Thomas Cromwell. For Cranmer, things were certainly moving in the right direction, even if reform moved slowly.

There was still another document of significant importance that was drawn up during those years – a *Confession of Faith* for the Church of England. Archbishop Cranmer's desire was for this document to dispel discord and bring harmony among his clergy. Initially, Thomas wrote it for his own Diocese of Canterbury. But there was just the possibility that other bishops in the Church of England might follow his example. Instead of many different documents, he proposed to draw up only one to which all could subscribe.

He consulted with his bishops and gave them a copy of his forty-two articles of faith. He wanted their advice before presenting them to the king. Then in May 1552, Cranmer was asked to bring the list of articles before King Edward and members of his council. After scrutiny, it was returned to him to make the necessary revisions that had been suggested. Shortly after, Thomas sent it back to the council for the king's signature, in the hope that the Church would soon experience a period of peace and quiet. Due to recurring bouts of illness, Edward didn't sign the document until June the following year. A month later, disaster befell the Royal household.

Early evening, on the 6th July 1553, a knock came to the door of the archbishop's study.

'Yes, come in,' called Thomas. The door opened. It was one of his chaplains.

'My Lord Archbishop,' he said. 'I have just received word. Your presence at Greenwich Palace is requested immediately.'

Something bad has happened to the king, thought Thomas.

'Have my horse ready,' he ordered. As the man hurried from the doorway, Thomas grabbed his Bible and made for the king's bedside.

The Beginning of the End

He was only fifteen years old. Now he was dead. It was tuberculosis[1] that killed the young King of England in the end. His health had failed from a bout of measles and smallpox that he had contracted in the summer of 1552, but he never recovered fully from those. By the winter, Edward was too weak to fight off the disease. It eventually killed him the following summer. He died on 6th July, 1553.

At Greenwich Palace, Archbishop Cranmer left King Edward's bedchamber in sorrow. He had seen his fair share of tragedy in the Royal Family over the years. It is so painful to lose someone so cherished and so young.

There was fear that the king's death would put an end to the Protestant reforms that had been introduced during his reign. The powerful and ambitious Duke of Northumberland, John Dudley, had devised a shrewd plan that would fend off any attempts by the Catholics

---

1. *Tuberculosis* is a terrible disease that usually affects the lungs, making it very difficult to breathe. It can cause its sufferers to cough up blood.

to unravel the changes. It also placed him closer to the throne of England – a nice little bonus for him or the real reason for his plan? As King Edward's mentor over the years, Northumberland knew that he could convince the ailing boy to make a will that would help secure a Protestant future for his realm.

Northumberland's first move was to have his son, Guildford Dudley, marry Lady Jane Grey. She was a descendant of Henry VIII's sister who was called Mary. This meant Lady Jane Grey had a place in the line of succession to the throne of England, even if it was only a tenuous one. The king did not want a Catholic to inherit his crown and so he was very favourable to Northumberland's 'device' for keeping England a Protestant nation.

Henry VIII's will declared that either of his two daughters, Mary, or Elizabeth, should succeed to the throne of England if his son Edward died without having children. But Edward's new will sought to override his father's wishes. Instead, Lady Jane Grey would inherit the Crown. She was a staunch Protestant, and this was pleasing to Edward. She would keep England on the path of true religion.

When the king's council received the document, they were not in favour of it. The judges didn't like it either. But when they were summoned before the king, they capitulated due to his insistence. Signatures were needed to make it binding, so they signed it. There was only one more name to put on it. The man who was committed to the royal supremacy, Thomas Cranmer.

'My Lord Archbishop, you must sign this document,' demanded Northumberland. 'It is the only way to protect the future of England.'

'I gave assurances to King Henry that I would support the succession of either daughter, even if it is Mary. I know that her allegiance lies with Rome. But I ...'

'My Lord Archbishop,' interrupted Northumberland, 'look how far we have come during the reign of our present king.' If Mary becomes Queen of England, you can be sure she will reverse all our good and righteous reforms. And many will face the Tower or worse, even you, Archbishop.'

'If that is the will of God, then so be it,' said the archbishop.

Northumberland paused for a moment to collect his thoughts, then said, 'let me assure you, Archbishop, that His Majesty's judiciary has deemed this document legal. You would do well not to offend the king's wishes. As a matter of fact, the king is begging you not to oppose him in this matter.'

And there it was. The arrow hit the mark and the opposition weakened in Cranmer. The judges legalised it, and the king insisted on it. Thomas relented and subscribed to the king's will. He knew deep down that Princess Mary would not welcome the changes imposed by her half-brother. Trouble was coming, he was sure of that.

Now that Edward was dead, the details of his will were put into effect. Four days after King Edward VI's death, Lady Jane Grey was crowned Queen of England. The Duke of Northumberland wanted her to proclaim his son Guildford as king. But she mustered up the courage to decline his suggestion. It was obvious to Northumberland that she would need a little bit more persuasion, but that was for another day. Let her get settled into her new role and perhaps she would change her mind. He would try again later.

However, Queen Jane did not have an opportunity to get settled into her new position. Those opposed to Princess Mary's succession had underestimated the esteem and respect that the nation of England had for her. Northumberland had not allowed for public opinion in his plan. The people were not convinced that the succession of Lady Jane Grey was entirely lawful. Plus, the public saw the Duke of Northumberland as a greedy and ambitious man. They didn't like him at all. It was easy to oppose him and back the princess in her quest.

Events moved swiftly. Princess Mary arrived in London with an ever-growing army of supporters in a bid to take over the Crown. As far as she was concerned, it was rightfully hers anyway. She ousted Jane from her position as Queen of England and sent the deposed monarch to the Tower of London, along with the Duke of Northumberland.

Princess Mary was enthroned on 19th July, 1553. Queen Jane had ruled for only nine days. The Privy Council issued a letter on 20th July declaring Mary as the rightful Queen of England. Archbishop Cranmer signed it. His next business was to bury the recently deceased King Edward. Huge numbers of dignitaries and common folk gathered at Westminster Abbey on 8th August to mourn the passing of the young monarch.

The new sovereign did not waste any time in showing her determination to eliminate the Protestant faith from England. It seemed like only moments after her coronation, she recruited and dispatched agents to gather up men and women of Protestant persuasion for imprisonment in the Tower. Leading churchmen were especially targeted for incarceration, especially Archbishop Cranmer. Thomas sat at his desk in Lambeth Palace to write to his continental friends who were living and ministering in England. He said the same thing in each letter he wrote, urging them to leave England in haste. *'I exhort you,'* he began, *'to withdraw yourself from the malice of your God's enemies into some place where God is most truly served. And that you will do, do it with speed, lest by your own folly you fall into the persecutors' hands. And the Lord send his Holy Spirit to lead and guide you, wheresoever you go.'*

Despite pleas from his friends to take his own advice, Cranmer did not think it fitting for a man of his position to flee for safety's sake. He was quite prepared to face any punishment for the reforms he had brought to bear on a corrupt and heretical Church of England. When his friend, Nicholas Ridley, heard that Cranmer was staying put in England, he wrote to him. *'If you, O man of God, do purpose to live in this realm, prepare and arm yourself to die: for there is no appearance or likelihood of any other thing, except you will deny your Master Christ.'* Ridley was among the first to be imprisoned for a sermon that he preached against the legitimacy of Mary's claim to the throne.

False rumours and accusations were soon manifest whereby Cranmer supposedly restored the Catholic Mass in his Cathedral in Canterbury. He also apparently offered to say Mass in St Paul's before Queen Mary. These things were not true. They distressed Cranmer so much that he wrote a statement to counter the falsehoods that were circulating.

At his study desk once again, he picked up his quill, dipped it in his ink well, and started writing. *'Although I have been well exercised these twenty years in suffering and bearing evil rumours, reports, and lies, and have not been much grieved on account of them but have borne all things quietly: yet when untrue reports and lies turn to the hindrance of God's Truth, then they are not to be tolerated or to be suffered. Wherefore this is to signify to the world that it was not I that did set up the Mass in Canterbury. And as for offering myself to say Mass before the Queen's Highness at Paul's, or in any other place, I never did it, as Her Grace well knows. But if Her Grace will give me leave, I will prove against all that would say the contrary, that all that is said in the Holy Communion set forth by the most innocent and godly prince, King Edward the Sixth, in his court of Parliament, is conformable to that order that our Saviour Christ did both observe and command to be observed.'*

He paused for a moment to give his writing finger a moment's rest. Then he declared in the statement that he was keen to prove by public debate, if necessary, that '*all the doctrine and religion set forth by our Sovereign Lord King Edward the Sixth is more pure and according to God's Word than any other that have been used in England in a thousand years.*' Thomas intended to pin the statement on to the door of St Paul's Cathedral, as was customary when seeking debate about a religious issue. Martin Luther did that in Wittenburg and look what happened after that! Instead, Cranmer gave a copy of it to one of his fellow bishops, who in turn had copies made and passed it around. Soon it was copied and circulated everywhere. He was called to appear before the Court of Star Chamber to give account of his statement. But it was simply a ruse. Cranmer was transferred to the Tower of London on the charge of treason against the Crown. It was the end of his freedom.

The Duke of Northumberland, John Dudley, had already been beheaded for his plot against the queen. From Mary's point of view, Archbishop Cranmer had nullified the marriage of her mother; overthrown her religion; and taken part in the recent conspiracy against her which left the throne to Lady Jane Grey. Undoubtedly, it was only a matter of time before Archbishop Cranmer would meet the same immediate end. If the executioner's blade was sharp, it would be swift and painless. But if not, it would be slow and excruciating, as in the case of Thomas Cromwell. It did not matter to the queen if the blade was as blunt as a spoon, she was resolute that Thomas Cranmer was going to die.

The date for his hearing was set. Along with Lady Jane Grey and a few others, Archbishop Cranmer would be put on trial on 13th November, 1553. When the day of the trial arrived, it was not surprising the speed at which the accused were found guilty of treason and sentenced to death.

Three months later, Lady Jane Grey waved goodbye to her husband, Guildford Dudley, from the small window of her cell in the Tower of London. He was on his way to the block on Tower Green, the spot preferred for public executions. Shortly after, she watched his head and body being wheeled back in a cart to the Tower chapel. Then it was her turn to face the executioner's axe. She gripped her *Book of Common Prayer* tightly in her hand. She prayed the whole way of her final journey in this world to the scaffold at Tower Green. She removed her blindfold and dark robe that was the usual attire for the condemned. An onlooker grabbed her by the hand and helped her on to the scaffold where the dreaded block sat. The wood was darkly stained with the blood of victims of past beheadings. As she knelt, she turned to the executioner and begged, 'Pray, dispatch me quickly.' It was his job to oblige her. It was over in the blink of an eye.

This was the outcome for those who were steadfast in their desire to see reform in the Church. Many were hunted down and murdered by some bloody means. If the queen's agents found any Bibles, they were dipped in the victim's blood. These became known as the Martyr's Bibles and a rare few are still in existence today. During her five-year reign, she murdered over two hundred men and women who professed a Protestant faith in Christ.

By the laws of the Church, the Archbishop of Canterbury could not be executed until he suffered public humiliation and then expulsion from his priestly Orders. This would take time. Although Thomas stood trial alongside Lady Jane Grey, he would not face execution until sometime later. It was only a momentary reprieve from death. And the road to death would take its toll on the gentle archbishop.

Imprisoned

Thomas was placed in a cell in the Tower of London, with Hugh Latimer, the former Bishop of Worcester, Nicholas Ridley, the Bishop of London, and a man called John Bradford who was a local Protestant preacher. The four men wanted to strengthen their faith in the Lord Jesus Christ, so they had long Bible studies together and they prayed together. It was a great help and comfort to these godly men in their hour of need.

Then one day in early April 1544, a jailer came to their cell, accompanied by soldiers in armour and huge pykes in their hands. 'You are being moved,' the jailer gruffly said.

'Where to?' asked Nicholas

'Oxford,' came the reply.

'All of us?' asked Bradford.

'Not you,' answered the jailer tersely.

The door of the cell then swung open. The soldiers grabbed Cranmer, Latimer and Ridley, pulled them to their feet and bound them.

'Where in Oxford?' asked Cranmer, as the restraints were pulled tightly round his wrists.

'The Bocardo,' said the jailer. 'Enough questions.' He looked at the soldiers and with a nod of the head, the men were escorted briskly out of their cell. The Bocardo was part of the northern gate of the city of Oxford. From there, the men would be brought individually before the religious scholars of Oxford and Cambridge, to debate their views about the Lord's Supper. They were never engaged in debate, but rather they were there to be ridiculed, humiliated, and belittled by their peers.

Cranmer also found out that his charge of treason was altered to a charge of heresy. Queen Mary was determined to see the archbishop burned at the stake as a heretic. Thomas had a strange sense of comfort in the change of the charge against him. He was no longer accused of any actions against the queen that he allegedly had undertaken, but for teaching the truth of Christ from the Bible – a much more noble and worthy cause to lay down his life for, he thought.

St Mary's Church in Oxford was the scene for Cranmer's first appearance before the Cambridge and Oxford *Divines* as they were known, who had been gathered to determine his guilt of heresy. They sat in the stalls of the choir and Cranmer was brought before them. The chairman of the tribunal handed Thomas a document that contained a list of sixteen articles stating how he had broken the laws of the Church. They wanted him to agree with these articles and sign his name to them. Thomas took the document and read it carefully a few times. In his opinion they were all contrary to the Word of God and he would not sign them. He was given the opportunity to put his objections in writing and debate them the following week.

On Monday 16th April, Cranmer was brought to Exeter College in Oxford. He was taken to a room where several religious scholars and scribes were seated round a table. Thomas stood before them. The chairman of the meeting began by stating that the point of the meeting was not so much to hear what the good archbishop should say about the sacrament, but rather it was to discredit his reformed and Protestant understanding of the Lord's Supper.

'Well, then, this is a waste of time,' said Archbishop Cranmer. 'If you have already made up your minds before the truth is heard, then this debate is useless.' It was one of the few occasions that he was able to say something without being rudely interrupted. And he made a good point, which was sadly ignored by those gathered, nonetheless. What followed could only be described as a disorderly display of ignorance and arrogance on the part of his accusers. The archbishop was bombarded with question after question, barely having time to finish his answer before another question was asked or another point made. Thomas was too well read to be caught out by any of the scholars. In fact, he thought they didn't understand what they were talking about and were very childish too. He was constantly chided when speaking, and sometimes they made so much noise that Thomas could not be heard. It was as if they were not interested in what he had to say. Well, of course they weren't! They just wanted to disgrace and taunt him. Irrespective of how he was treated, Archbishop Cranmer was courteous throughout it all. The dreadful ordeal lasted nearly six hours. It was exhausting for the sixty-five-year-old Archbishop.

There was another appearance at St Mary's in Oxford, only this time Cranmer was accompanied by Latimer and Ridley. The chair of the tribunal asked if they would recant their beliefs, but they would not. They were condemned as heretics and sentenced to death. They would languish in the cells of the Bocardo until the time of their execution.

In the meantime, the Queen of England continued to hunt down and persecute anyone who adhered to the Protestant faith. It was always Mary's intention to reverse the Reformation in England as far as she could. A way to strengthen the link with the Holy Roman Empire was an alliance with Spain through marriage. In the summer of 1554, Philip II of Spain (the son of Charles V, the Holy Roman Emperor and King of Spain) arrived in England. Four days later he met Queen Mary for the first time. The following day, they had a magnificent wedding in Winchester Cathedral. It was fortunate that they liked the look of each other (at least at the start!). It didn't really matter though, as the motivation for their wedlock was power, not love. Philip was then pronounced King of England, strengthening his influence in Europe.

There was opposition to the marriage from the queen's most trusted advisor, Bishop Stephen Gardiner. When Mary came to the throne of England, Gardiner was released from his imprisonment and reinstated as the Bishop of Winchester. He even had the honour of placing the crown on Mary's head at her coronation. Mary was a devout catholic, and he admired her. But he did not like her union with Philip. Gardiner felt strongly that the king would only treat England as an outpost of his father's vast empire. He was not alone in his scepticism. The English people did not care for an alliance with Spain.

As the months passed, Mary was successful in reconciling England to Rome once again. But then came the death of the queen's trusted advisor, Bishop Stephen Gardiner. There was no doubt that he was a key figure in Mary's counter-reformation. She would miss his wise counsel, especially at a time when she needed it most. However, the work to undo Archbishop Cranmer's reforms continued.

News of the reconciliation with Rome reached Cranmer in the Tower. It broke his heart. A fleeting thought entered Cranmer's mind: *was it all for nothing?* Then he gave himself a good talking to — *of course it wasn't! The Lord God is in control of all things, and will work his purposes out, as he has promised in his Word. As for me, I shall put my trust in Christ, my Saviour, and my God.*

The days turned to weeks and then to months. His resolve waned under the strain of incarceration. The food was grim, but it kept him alive. Latimer and Ridley were in different cells by now. Occasionally they would write to each other and have a servant bring the correspondence to them. They were glad of any words that might encourage them to stay strong and keep the faith.

By the autumn of 1555, papal authority had put the Catholic bishop, James Brooks, in charge of Thomas Cranmer's final trial in St Mary's Church in Oxford. It was not his responsibility to dispute any of Cranmer's views, but simply to enquire if he would recant and return his allegiance to Rome. Cranmer was not prepared to acknowledge that the pope had any jurisdiction in the realm of England. Furthermore, he did not teach anything false concerning the sacrament of the Lord's Supper. The trial finished that afternoon. Brooks was required to give a report of the proceedings to the pope, who would then decide what to do with Cranmer.

During this time, Thomas wrote to Queen Mary. He pointed out that her oath to the pope was not consistent with her oath to the realm of England as the supreme head of the Church of England. He also reminded her that as an advocate of royal supremacy, he was still her obedient servant. He was prepared to go to Rome to plead his case there: *'and I trust that God shall put in my mouth to defend his truth there as well as here,'* he wrote.

Thomas never made a trip to Rome to plead his case before the pope. Soon after his trial in St Mary's he learned the awful truth that his friends, Hugh Latimer, and Nicholas Ridley, were to be burned at the stake together. On 16th October 1555, they were led by armed guards through the Oxford streets that were lined with onlookers, to the place of martyrdom. As they passed under the window of Thomas's cell, Nicholas looked up to see if he could catch a glimpse of his mentor and friend. But a Spanish friar called Petro de Soto had visited Thomas with the express purpose of getting him to recant. Thomas was engaged in discussion with the friar when Nicholas looked for his presence at the window. Seeing that Thomas was not there, he turned to see if Latimer was not too far behind him. He could see his old friend following along.

As soon as Thomas was free from the friar, he made for the small cell window. He could see the sight of execution and the backs of his friends as they arrived there. Thomas fell on his knees in prayer. 'Oh Lord God Almighty, please strengthen these your good and faithful servants with strength and courage as they face death for your name's sake. Be pleased to welcome them into your eternal and glorious presence when this wicked deed is done,' he begged.

The blacksmith placed an iron belt around the waists of the two bishops as they stood back-to-back at the stake. Bundles of sticks, also known as faggots, were placed around their feet and lower bodies. A soldier placed bags of gunpowder around their necks to speed up the kill. The frail and elderly Latimer turned his head and said to Ridley, 'Be of good comfort, Master Ridley, and play the man. We shall this day light such a candle by God's grace in England as I trust shall never be put out!'

The fire was lit, and the flames began to rise around the men's feet. Latimer bathed his hands in the fire as it climbed up his legs to his body, and then he died. It was a very quick death. But the flames could not proceed beyond the thick woodpile around Ridley's legs so that the main trunk of his body was unsinged. In agony he begged for help to release the wood and allow the flames to rise. He shouted out, 'I cannot burn!' One of the onlookers pulled the upper faggots away to allow the flames to consume the bishop. But he bent his head forward to the flames and the bags of gunpowder round his neck did the rest. In the Bocardo cell, Thomas Cranmer fell to his knees and wept. The punishment inflicted upon his brothers in Christ were more painful to him than death itself. His time to die would soon come. Would the leader of the English Reformation remain steadfast to the end, like those whose martyrdom he had just witnessed? Was it possible that the two years he suffered imprisonment and fierce persecution could weaken the strength and resilience that he possessed during all those years in the service of two kings and one Queen of England?

Would his service as an ambassador of the King of Kings remain absolute to the end?

In the days that followed, he wrote to a friend: '*I have not deemed it right to pass over one thing which I have learned by experience, namely, that God never shines forth more brightly, and pours out the beams of his mercy and consolation, or of strength and firmness of spirit, more clearly or impressively upon the minds of his people, than when they are under the most extreme pain and distress, that he may then more specially show himself to be the God of his people when he seems to have altogether forsaken them; then raising them up when they think he is bringing them down and laying them low. I pray to God that I may endure to the end.*' Indeed, the end was approaching.

Recant and Die!

Thomas missed everyone and everything. He longed to see his wife Margarete and his children. He prayed for them every night. He missed his friends, Hugh and Nicholas in particular. And he missed his books and writing. Cut off from the outside world, alone, without human interaction and fellowship, can seriously damage a person's emotional, spiritual and mental health. The devil makes sure of it! The good archbishop had been imprisoned for two and a half years and his resolve was ebbing away. That was exactly what the establishment was hoping for. His captors wanted a recantation of his Protestant faith to parade before the nation.

In order to relieve the Bocardo bailiffs of their responsibility for Cranmer's care over the winter, he was transferred from the prison in December 1555, to take up residence with the Dean of Christ Church in Oxford. It came not a moment too soon. At Christ Church, Thomas received cordial hospitality from his host for the two months that he was there. A comfortable bed, good food, clean clothes, books, stimulating conversation with students and visitors to the Dean's university – it was amazing! Occasionally he even played a game of bowls with anyone who would accept the challenge.

It so happened that another Spanish friar called Juan de Villagarcia had been invited to teach at the university. The dean thought it might be good for him to meet with Cranmer and engage him in some of the controversial discussions that condemned the good archbishop to a fiery demise. Perhaps the friar could get Cranmer to change his mind and recant. De Villagarcia turned out to be a worthy adversary in debating the issues, but Cranmer remained resolute, at least for now.

The papists employed several tactics to unsettle and deflate Cranmer's confidence in the truth of God's Word. Of course, they sensed that he was tired and dejected from countless debates and discussions; from isolation, and from the deaths of his friends and supporters of biblical reform in the Church of England. At Christ Church it was obvious that he was enjoying the freedoms that had been taken away from him over the past couple of years. All he had to do was say he was wrong, take it all back, declare allegiance to Rome and he'd be free. But what if he didn't? Well, that one was easy to answer. Loneliness, hopelessness and death were nothing to look forward to.

When Thomas was returned to the Bocardo at the start of February 1556, attempts were made in the following weeks to get him to recant. It was then that

Thomas began to falter. His prolonged suffering was too much to bear and finally he gave in to his tormentor's demands. The Spanish Friars harangued the archbishop until they got him to sign a recantation. But it was dismissed as insincere and ignored. They needed to keep at it. He signed another, but that one wasn't good enough either.

Queen Mary was adamant that the archbishop was to undergo a ceremony of humiliation post trial. This was overseen by Thomas Thirlby, the Bishop of Westminster, and Edmund Bonner, the Bishop of London. Bonner was looking forward to the opportunity to degrade Cranmer. On the other hand, Thirlby had a more uncomfortable demeanour about him. He had known friendship from Cranmer in the past and did not relish the task as his colleague did. On this occasion, Christ Church in Oxford would play host to the barbarism. The archbishop was presented before those who had gathered to witness his degradation. Bonner began by expressing the fairness with which Cranmer's case had been heard at Rome. Thomas could not help himself: 'O Lord, what lies be these!' he cried out. He was quickly silenced.

They dressed him in the vestments of his church office. But his clothes and his bishop's hat were made of rotten canvas. The scene was like that of his Master when Jesus had a robe thrown about his shoulders and a crown of thorns placed on his head, mocking him as King of the Jews. Cranmer had abuse hurled at him by

Bonner, who loved every poisoned moment of it. Then they stripped the vestments from his back. They shaved his head and they put a poor man's gown on him and a cap on his head. And there he stood, disgraced and dejected. When the humiliation was over, Thomas was taken back to the Bocardo.

Bishop Bonner kept pushing for a *proper* recantation when he visited Thomas in his cell the following day. But it was not until later in February 1556 that he got what he was looking for. The gentle scholar put his name to a prepared statement, renouncing all heresies and teachings that conflicted with the true faith of the Roman Catholic Church. The statement also acknowledged the pope in Rome as the supreme head of the Church on earth. How low and broken Thomas must have felt, to sign such a document. Bonner printed it in Latin. The religious men were so excited that they had many copies of the recantation reproduced and handed out. However, because it was printed in Latin which ordinary people could not understand, and witnessed by two Spanish Friars, not English (remember, the general public wasn't that agreeable towards Spain), many believed it to be a hoax. The Privy Council ordered that all copies of the publication be gathered up and burned. This was achieved on 13th March 1556.

Five days later, another statement of recantation was put before Cranmer. It described him as the evil mastermind behind all the wrongs that had befallen the Church and Realm of England over the years of the Reformation. It was written in a way that would discredit his leadership and remove any last ounce of dignity he had left. It worked. Thomas gave in and signed for the last time. Some of his opponents thought a pardon for Cranmer would allow them to take further advantage of the situation in terms of propaganda. Queen Mary, however, wanted Cranmer dead. She received his recantation on 19th March and gave the orders for his death by fire to happen on 21st March 1556.

The night before his death, Thomas knelt to pray not only for himself, but for his enemies too: 'O God the Father of heaven, have mercy upon us, miserable sinners.' His voice was soft and deliberate. 'O God the Son, Redeemer of the world, have mercy upon us, miserable sinners. O God the Holy Spirit, proceeding from the Father and the Son, have mercy upon us, miserable sinners.' He paused to gently clear his throat. Then he continued: 'In all time of tribulation; in all time of wealth; in the hour of death, and in the day of judgement, good Lord, deliver us and hear us: that it may please you to bring into the way of truth all who have erred and are deceived: that it may please you to strengthen such as do stand; and to comfort and help the weak hearted; and to raise up those that fall; and finally to beat down Satan under our feet: that it may please you to succour, help and comfort all that are in danger, necessity and tribulation: that it may please you to forgive our enemies, persecutors and slanderers and to turn their hearts: that it may please you to give us true repentance; to forgive us all our sins, negligences and ignorances; and to endue us with the grace of your Holy Spirit to amend our lives according to your holy Word'[1].

The Bible says that if we confess our sins, truly and earnestly, God is faithful and just and will forgive us our sins and cleanse us from all unrighteousness. At his point of weakness and true humility, Thomas knew the abundant grace of God and it overwhelmed him to the point of tears. Out of weakness, this man of God was made strong.

The day of his execution was stormy. The rain was lashing down outside his cell window while the strong wind bent the branches of the trees close to the northern gate of Oxford. The crowd began to gather early that morning. The queen was unsure of their mood concerning the archbishop's execution, so she ordered that there should be a significant security presence in the city.

For the last time, Thomas was brought to St Mary's Church in Oxford and escorted to a seat opposite the pulpit. The queen had instructed the Provost of Eton, Dr Cole, to preach Cranmer's funeral sermon in the presence of the condemned man. Tears flowed down

---

1. These beautiful and sincere words are found in Cranmer's *Book of Common Prayer* and are part of the Litany, also known as the prayer of General Supplication.

Thomas's face as he listened and prayed throughout the sermon. When the sermon was over, Dr Cole entreated Cranmer to address the crowd and remove any doubt that he was a catholic again. Thomas rose to his feet. He was dressed in a dirty robe and cap. He pulled the cap off his head and encouraged the congregation to pray with him. Then he began to speak to them, exhorting them to care more for the world to come than the present one; to obey the King and Queen of England, out of fear for the Lord; to do good to everyone and to take care of the poor. He encouraged them to take heed of these things after he was gone.

There was nothing disagreeable with what Cranmer said so far. Dr Cole was quite satisfied with the proceedings. Neither he, nor the people who had gathered in St Mary's that day, were aware that this was only an introduction to the real ending that Thomas had in mind. For that last night in his cell at the Bocardo, he had determined to publicly repent; not for those things which he did to reform the Church in the realm of England, but for denying them! He would publicly proclaim his full agreement with the Reformation in England and with its focus on faithful biblical teaching.

'Now I come to the great thing that troubles my conscience,' he said with composure and strength in his voice. The congregation listened intently. This was it – the moment that Archbishop Thomas Cranmer would openly confess his true catholic faith, they thought.

'I have written things that are contrary to the truth, and I renounce them all. I reject all those things which I have written with my hand that have been against truth and what I believed in my heart. I was afraid to die, and I wanted to save my life if I could. But all such statements that I have written or signed with my own hand since my public humiliation, they are absolutely untrue.' Gasps could be heard from the nave of the building. He raised his voice slightly. 'And as my hand has offended my heart with writing such things, my hand shall be punished first, because if I am to be burned, it shall be burned first of all. And as for the pope,' his voice rising as the noise of the congregation grew, 'I reject him as Christ's enemy and anti-Christ, with all his false teaching. And as for the sacrament of the Lord's Supper ...'

Well, Thomas couldn't be heard any more. Once the crowd realised that he was recanting his recantations, they were furious with him. He was ordered to be quiet and say no more, and to reflect on his previous recantations, and stop all the pretence! This allowed Thomas to say a little bit more. 'I have always loved plain speaking, so I am very sorry.' Then quickly he cried out, 'and as for the sacrament of the Lord's Supper, I believe what I have taught in my *Book of Common Prayer* is true and it's truth shall stand at the last day before the judgement of God!'

'Enough!' thundered Dr Cole, his face red with anger. He looked at the bailiffs and barked, 'Take him away!' They grabbed Thomas and dragged him as quickly as they could out of St Mary's and to the site of his torture. It was the same place where he witnessed the terrible deaths of Latimer and Ridley six months prior. He took off his dark worn-out robe to reveal a long grubby shirt that fell to his feet. His long flowing beard was down to his chest and gave him an aura of dignity.

The bystanders looked on as an iron belt was placed around his waist clamping him to the wooden stake. Then the faggots were lit. The fire rose quickly around Thomas. He held his right hand into the flames and kept it there until it was burned to a stump. All the while he kept shouting, 'this hand has offended!' He did not move even as the flames engulfed him. He lifted his eyes to the heavens and repeatedly cried, 'Lord Jesus, receive my spirit!' until his voice was gone. Throughout the whole horrific ordeal, Thomas knew the peace of God within him. They could kill his body, but his soul belonged to Jesus Christ.

On the morning of 21st March, 1556, in the city of Oxford, England, Thomas Cranmer gasped his last smoky breath on earth. He was the servant of kings. But much more than that; Thomas Cranmer was the servant of the King of King's, Jesus Christ. Cranmer's heartfelt desire was to see the people of England come to a true knowledge and love of God and his Son Jesus Christ, through faithful Bible teaching and reformed biblical liturgy. And his legacy can be seen in the millions of Christians worldwide who still use his *Book of Common Prayer* today.

Thomas Cranmer
Timeline

1489   Thomas Cranmer born on 2nd July.

1514   Awarded his Master of Arts degree.

1516   Resigned from Jesus College and married Joan.

1517   Joan Cranmer died in childbirth. Cranmer reinstated as a professor at Jesus College.

1520   Thomas ordained priest in the Church of England.

1521   Granted his Bachelor of Divinity degree.

1526   Became Doctor of Divinity.

1529   Dinner at Waltham on 2nd August with Dr Stephen Gardiner and Dr Edward Fox.

1530   Became King of England's envoy to Rome.

1531   Became Archdeacon of Taunton then royal chaplain.

1532   Became the king's ambassador in residence to the Court of the Holy Roman Emperor. Married again.

1533   Became the Archbishop of Canterbury. Annulled the marriage of King Henry VIII to Catherine of Aragon. Crowned Anne Boleyn Queen of England.

1534   The Act of Supremacy declared Henry VIII the supreme head of the Church of England.

1535   The Dissolution of the Monasteries began.

1536   Cranmer preached in St Paul's churchyard, attacking the papacy and purgatory!
Cranmer annulled the marriage of Henry VIII and Anne Boleyn.
The *Ten Articles* were written by the king and revised by Cranmer. Plague breaks out in London.
19th May, Anne Boleyn beheaded at the Tower.
30th May, Henry VIII married Jane Seymour.

1537   12th October, Edward VI is born. Jane Seymour died twelve days after giving birth to Edward.

1538   The Great Bible was published.

1539   Act of *Six Articles* passed.

1540   6th January, Henry VIII married Anne of Cleves.
9th July, Henry VIII divorced Anne of Cleves.

28th July, Thomas Cromwell executed at Tower Hill. King Henry married Catherine Howard.

1541   Cranmer contributed to the Preface of the English Bible.

1542   The Plot of the Prebendaries.
13th February, Catherine Howard beheaded.

1543   Cranmer started to write his *Book of Homilies*.
12th July, King Henry VIII married Catherine Parr.
The Plot of the Privy Council.

1545   Archbishop Cranmer's *English Litany* published.

1547   28th January, King Henry VIII died at the age of 55.
20th February Archbishop Cranmer crowned Edward VI King of England at Westminster Abbey.
The *Book of Homilies* is published.
Act of *Six Articles* was repealed, as was clergy celibacy.

1548   Cranmer abandoned belief in Transubstantiation for a reformed position on the Lord's Supper.
Cranmer brought first draft of *Book of Common Prayer* before the bishops.

1549   First Act of Uniformity.
Peasants uprising in the North of England.

1550   Archbishop published 'A Defence of the True and Catholic Doctrine of the Sacrament'.

1552   Second Act of Uniformity.
Cranmer submitted 42 Articles to council.

1553   6 July, King Edward VI died. Lady Jane Grey became Queen of England for nine days.
14th September, Cranmer arrested for treason against Queen Mary.

1554   12th February, Lady Jane Grey and husband Guildford Dudley executed.

1555   16 October, Archbishop Cranmer witnessed Bishops Latimer and Ridley burned at stake in Oxford.

1556   Archbishop Thomas Cranmer signed final recantation of reformed beliefs.
21st March, he recanted the recantations! Burned at the stake in Oxford.

Thinking Further Topics

1. The Dinner Party

Thomas Cranmer just happened to be at the same place as Edward Fox and Stephen Gardiner at Waltham in 1529. Was this just coincidence, or do you believe that God guides events and people to bring about his purposes? Read the Book of Ruth and Matthew 1:1-16. Change doesn't happen overnight.

2. A Very Big Problem

Cranmer did not think that the pope had the authority to excuse people from obeying some of the laws of God. Was he right, or should Thomas have obeyed the authority of the pope in Rome? Read Hebrews 1:1-2, John 14:26 and Mark 7:8 to get you started in your thinking about who's in authority in the Church.

3. A Trip to Rome

Thomas was frustrated that he could not get the church authorities in Italy to listen to him. Do you ever get frustrated when you have something to say and no one will listen to you? How should you react when this happens? Read Colossians 4:5-6 and Galatians 5:22-23.

4. In the King's Service

Thomas thought long and hard before accepting any new truth. Are you like that, or do you prefer to believe what your friends tell you to believe? Read Colossians 1:9-10 and Romans 12:2.

5. The Promotion

Cranmer felt powerless when his wife died. Have you ever known this feeling of powerlessness in the face of death? If so, I am so very sorry that you have had to experience this even at a young age. Death is not the end and will not be victorious over us. Read 1 Corinthians 15:55-58 and Romans 8:38-39.

6. The Ultimatum
Cranmer prayed for the new princess Elizabeth that she would grow up to confess Christ as her Lord and Saviour. Have you ever been ashamed in the company of others to say that you are a Christian? If so, why? Read Luke 9:23-26, 2 Timothy 1:8-10 and 1 Peter 4:16.

7. The Queen's Advocate
The Church of England had amassed great wealth at the expense of the people. Was that right? Do you love money and hope to be rich when you get older? Read Acts 2:42-47 and 1 Timothy 6:6-10.

8. Cranmer's Bible
Cranmer's Bible was to be placed in every church throughout the England. Why was this important to Cranmer? Do you love the Bible and read it regularly? If not, why not? Read 2 Timothy 3:14–4:5.

9. A True Friend
Cranmer was persecuted by many people for his biblical reforms. Have you ever been persecuted as a follower of Jesus Christ? Did it come as a surprise to you? Read Hebrews 10:32-39 and 2 Thessalonians 1:3-10.

10. The King is Dead, Long Live the King
Cranmer wanted to take superstition out of the Lord's Supper by abandoning the teaching of transubstantiation and he created a new service of the Lord's Supper in his

Prayer Books. Have you ever thought why Christians celebrate the Lord's Supper? Read 1 Corinthians 11:17-34.

11. The New Prayer Book

It was important to Cranmer that the Church of England moved forward in unity. The Acts of Uniformity passed by King Edward's parliament helped this happen. Do you think unity is important in God's church? Read Ephesians 4:11-18 and Philippians 1:27-28.

12. The Beginning of the End

Queen Mary was a devout Roman Catholic. She was respected for her piety, but harboured great hatred in her heart for Archbishop Cranmer. Thomas did not feel the same way about the queen. Should we believe in Christ and hate people at the same time? Read Luke 6:27-36.

13. Imprisoned

Cranmer was imprisoned and news of the reconciliation with Rome broke his heart. The pain and suffering that he endured was it all for nothing? Has a difficult situation in your life made you doubt that God is involved in your life? Read Psalm 73:1-28.

14. Recant and Die!

The Church authorities took advantage of Cranmer's weakness in the last days of his life. He recanted of his reforms that were fuelled by his biblical faith in Christ. Have you ever renounced Jesus? Is there any chance of coming back from that? Read Luke 22:54-62 and John 21:15-19.

FACT FILE

The Mass

The Mass played a central role in the medieval church of Thomas Cranmer's day. In the Mass, the actual body of Christ was present by a real change of the bread. This was known as transubstantiation. God's grace was only available by eating the body of Christ that was sacrificed again by the priest.

The Reformers rejected this as unbiblical and untrue. For them, the saving power of the death and resurrection of Jesus was entirely God's work. The benefits of God's grace could only be received by trusting in the Lord who had made it all possible. The idea that a human priest could sacrifice Christ again, the Reformers believed was absurd and offensive to God.

Many Reformers died because they rejected the teaching behind the Mass and transubstantiation. It wasn't just a difference of opinion, as some may argue today. The Reformers' teaching struck at the very heart of what the medieval Catholic Church believed.

Authority in the Church

The Bible was never seen as the only source of authority in the medieval Church of sixteenth century England. At that time the papacy insisted that the teaching of the Church could also come from tradition as it developed over time. In other words, there were certain things that were handed down from generation to generation that were not written in the Bible, but the medieval Church taught as true. In fact, the Roman Catholic Church was the only organisation that could properly understand truth, and so the people needed to listen to what the Church said about God.

However, Reformers like Thomas Cranmer insisted on Scripture alone as the true authority for the Church and therefore the Church was to sit under the rule of Scripture. There was nothing more to add. The Church was simply to confess the teaching of the Bible.

The Reformers also believed that the Bible should be available to everyone in their own language. That's why Thomas Cranmer was so overjoyed when the Great Bible made its appearance in England. When the Bible was translated into modern languages such as German and English, it had a major impact on the Reformation. The Reformers denied that uneducated people could not understand the Bible for themselves. After all, many of the first disciples were unschooled fishermen (read Acts 4:1-13). With an English Bible, people could weigh up the teaching of the Church against the Scriptures and work out for themselves if what they were hearing was the truth (read Acts 17:10-12).

The Reformers also insisted that when the Bible was faithfully and obediently taught, God's voice was truly heard. They believed that God the Holy Spirit illumined the mind of the believer so that he or she could understand the Bible. The Holy Spirit also helped the believer to live a life that pleased the Lord, in the light of that Word.

Cranmer was annoyed with people who insisted that the services continued in Latin, because it was a language that the ordinary person in England did not understand. Unless the service was in English and could be understood, it was all meaningless to the ordinary churchgoer.

Shrines, images and saints

The Reformers believed that worshipping or praying to an image of a saint at a shrine in a church building was idolatry. Idolatry is worshipping someone or something in the place of the true and living God of the Bible. Saints could not answer prayers, nor could they put in a good word with 'the man upstairs'. Only God answers prayers, so why not pray to him directly? The second commandment was often quoted as the reason for destroying any shrines and images in churches (read Exodus 20:4-6).

Saints were not divine, and they certainly were not mediators between us and God, only Christ (read 1 Timothy 2:5). Therefore, saints had no power to heal and had no greater privilege than any other Christian. In fact, the Bible teaches that all Christians are saints, and the Reformers passionately upheld this view.

Pilgrimages[1] to holy sites to get closer to God were also folly to the Reformers. A person gets close to God through faith in Christ Jesus. The Bible says that Christ is seated at the right hand of God in Heaven (read Ephesians 1:20; Colossians 3:1). A Christian cannot get any closer to God than being in Christ, who is seated at God's right hand. Think about it – you can't get any closer to God than that!

House of Lords

In Britain, the House of Lords is one of the two Houses of Parliament. The other is the House of Commons where the politicians in government meet to discuss issues relating to the country.

In Cranmer's day, the House of Lords consisted mainly of members of the aristocracy (such as dukes) and high-ranking clergy in England, (such as bishops and archbishops). The members of the House of Lords also discuss important issues. The Lords can also approve laws and question the politicians about the work they are doing on behalf of the people they represent. The House of Lords today is made up of men and women from all walks of life, including some members of the aristocracy and clergy from the Church of England. The main responsibility was, and is, to improve the way the country is governed, making it a better place to live.

---

1. A pilgrimage is a journey that a religious person makes to a holy place, as an act of their devotion to God.

OTHER BOOKS IN THE
TRAIL BLAZERS SERIES

For a full list of Trail Blazers, please see our website:
www.christianfocus.com
All Trail Blazers are available as e-books

CHRISTIAN FOCUS PUBLICATIONS

Christian Focus   Christian Heritage   CF4K   Mentor

Christian Focus Publications publishes books for adults and children under its four main imprints: Christian Focus, CF4K, Mentor and Christian Heritage. Our books reflect our conviction that God's Word is reliable and Jesus is the way to know him, and live for ever with him.

Our children's publication list covers pre-school to early teens. We also publish personal and family devotional titles, biographies and inspirational stories that children will love.

From pre-school board books to teenage apologetics, we have it covered!

**Find us at our web page:
www.christianfocus.com**

CF4·K
Because you're never
too young to know Jesus